THE GOOD KIPLING

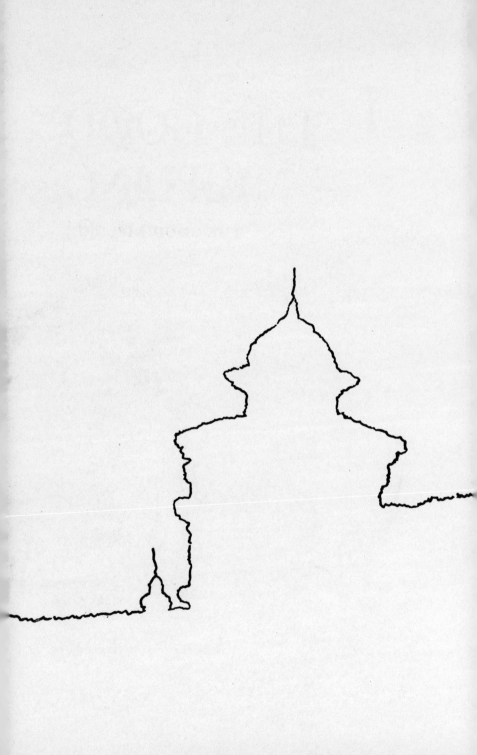

THE GOOD KIPLING

KIPLING

Studies in the Short Story

By
Elliot L. Gilbert

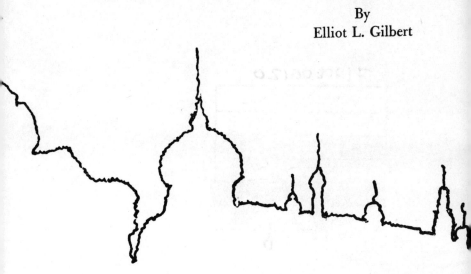

Manchester University Press

© 1972 Elliot L. Gilbert
All rights reserved

Published by
Manchester University Press
316-324 Oxford Road
Manchester M13 9NR

ISBN 0 7190 0478 0

Printed in Great Britain by
Lowe & Brydone (Printers) Ltd.
London N.W.10

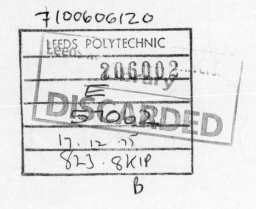
Design by Hal Stevens

FOR SANDRA

ACKNOWLEDGMENTS

This book was written with the help of a research grant from Cornell University and with grants-in-aid from Columbia University and the University of California. I would like to thank these institutions for their generous assistance. I wish also to thank Professor Robert M. Adams, who read the manuscript in its early stages and who made many valuable suggestions. Most of all, I wish to express my gratitude to my wife, Sandra, who has been devoted to this project from its beginnings, whose help has been generous and untiring, and whose contributions have been crucial. The book could not have been what it is without her.

Portions of a number of these chapters have appeared, in different form, in *PMLA*, *English Literature in Transition*, *Studies in Short Fiction*, the *Kipling Journal*, and in the anthology *Kipling and the Critics*, published by New York University Press. In addition, several paragraphs are reprinted from *Kenyon Review* and *Victorian Studies*. They all appear here by permission.

E.L.G.

Davis, California
January, 1971

CONTENTS

THE GOOD KIPLING

CHAPTER ONE ✳

"Not at all My Favorite Author"

"Not at all my favorite author," Karl Shapiro began, quoting from his *Bourgeois Poet* during a recent reading in California, "Kipling . . . "[1] But he could get no further into the passage than the mention of that name before he was obliged to stop and smile his acknowledgment of the audience's response. For the audience, consisting largely of college students and their teachers, with a sprinkling of faculty wives and bookish townspeople, was reacting—as it might have reacted to any other pleasant joke—with good-humored approval, with laughter, and even, finally, with applause.

The episode is an instructive one for readers interested in the present curious state of Rudyard Kipling's literary reputation. Among the more striking features of the Shapiro passage, for instance, is the poet's evident need, at least within the context of his poem, to apologize for the excerpt from Kipling which he quotes. The quotation itself is not the issue; Shapiro obviously approves of it. Rather, it is Kipling himself who is the object of the poet's defensiveness, a defensiveness which, on another occasion, George Orwell accounted for by suggesting that "a civilized person . . . would prefer not to feel that it was Kipling who had expressed his thought for him."[2] That this is true,

---

1. *The Bourgeois Poet* (New York, 1962), p. 57.
2. "Rudyard Kipling," *Essays* (New York, 1954), p. 134 (note).

and, moreover, that everyone knows this to be true, is borne out not only by Shapiro's apology but also by the audience's response to it. Shapiro, by saying "Not at all my favorite author," set up, with his irony and his inversion, a certain tension of curiosity which the next moment he discharged by mentioning the name "Kipling." The audience's laughter confirmed that no name could more appropriately have fulfilled the expectation aroused by the introductory phrase; confirmed, that is, that no writer today is more universally recognized to be in need of apology than Kipling.

Apologetic references of this sort to Kipling turn up with great frequency. In a well-known interview, for example, Ernest Hemingway, asked to list his literary forebears, produced a catalogue of thirty names, among them "Mark Twain, Flaubert, Stendahl, Turgenev, Tolstoi, Dostoievski, Chekhov, Andrew Marvell, John Donne, Maupassant, *the good Kipling*, [and] Thoreau . . ."[3] (italics mine). It is surely significant that of all the names mentioned by Hemingway only one seemed to demand a modifier—to demand, in other words, that its presence on the list be in some way justified. Kipling need not have been singled out in this way. Of the other artists mentioned, for instance, Mark Twain and Maupassant are also uneven writers. Yet when Hemingway listed these two, he was plainly not worried that, in the absence of a disclaimer, readers might suppose he had been influenced by the "bad" Mark Twain or the "bad" Maupassant. Only about Kipling did his uncharacteristic hesitancy produce the defensive adjective. Interestingly, there is a trace of a similar apologetic condescension in many of Ezra Pound's references to Kipling. In his *Guide to Kulchur*, for example,

---

3. George Plimpton, "Ernest Hemingway," *Writers at Work, Second Series* (New York, 1965), p. 227.

Pound wrote: "There is no mystery about the Cantos, they are the tale of the tribe—give Rudyard credit for his use of the phrase."[4] It is clear, both in his airy resort to the first name and in his suggestion that Kipling be credited more particularly with the phrase in question than with the idea represented by the phrase, that Pound preserves the somewhat contemptuous, apologetic tone of the "civilized person" who wants to be careful about the sort of people with whom he associates.

One obvious way to avoid the need for such apology is, of course, not to allude to or quote from Kipling at all. This, however, is harder than it seems, for Kipling, in a writing career which covered more than fifty years, had a remarkably widespread influence and produced some of the most unavoidable quotations in the English language. It might be supposed that such an uncanny ability to make a country's proverbs for it would have earned Kipling at least grudging respect among serious readers. But in fact his skill as a political phrase-maker, like his great and continuing popularity among ordinary book-buyers,[5] is often just what is held against him most; he is seen as a glib public relations expert for unsavory ideas, a flashy huckster for England's discredited imperial vision, "the voice"—to quote one particularly bitter critic—"of a dying hierarchy which, for all its cruelty, violence, and stupid complacency and reaction, [he] seeks to perpetuate."[6] It is, in other

---

4. Ezra Pound, *Guide to Kulchur* (New York, 1938), p. 194. For an exposition of this idea by Kipling, see his talk to the Royal Academy Dinner, May, 1906, published under the title "Literature" in *A Book of Words* (London, 1928), pp. 1-8. See also chapter six of the present study.

5. All his major works continue in print, and new anthologies of his poems and stories are regularly published in many languages, the French audience for his writings being especially large. For a comment on the Russian vogue for Kipling, see R[oger] L[ancelyn] G[reen], "Kipling in Russia," *Kipling Journal*, No. 143 (September 1962), 4.

6. H. E. Bates, *The Modern Short Story* (Boston, 1965), p. 111.

words, from the largely political and apparently propagan-
distic overtones of his work that "civilized persons" seem to
be trying to dissociate themselves when they apologize for
their frequent quotations from or references to Kipling's
poems, stories, and essays.

This persistent political approach to the author was a
problem from the first. In 1890, not yet twenty-five, Kipling
awoke one day, like Lord Byron before him, to find himself
famous. It was to be a troublesome sort of fame. For since
his principal subject matter happened to be the world of
contemporary India, he was quickly "taken up" by enthusi-
astic Anglo-Indians who had long and unsuccessfully been
seeking an official chronicler and spokesman and nearly
all of whom had a stake—whether political or merely sentimental is unimportant—in the perpetuation of the empire.
"One day," an early critic and member of India's Viceregal
Council declared, "a writer will arise—perhaps this young
poet is the destined man—who will make that nobler Anglo-
Indian world known as it really is. It will then be seen by
what a hard discipline of endurance our countrymen and
countrywomen in India are trained to do England's greatest work on earth . . . "[7] The moment the Kipling enthusi-
asts appeared, however, their enemies, as often as not their
political enemies, began to range themselves against the
young writer. One detractor, for example, depicted the
author as riding the crest of "a great back-wave" irresist-
ibly sweeping civilization "in the direction of absolute
barbarism" and as "adumbrating in his single person . . .
all that is most deplorable, all that is most retrograde and
savage, in the restless and uninstructed Hooliganism of
the time."[8]

7. Quoted by C. E. Carrington, *The Life of Rudyard Kipling* (New
York, 1955), p. 101.
8. Robert Buchanan, "The Voice of the Hooligan," *The Voice of
"The Hooligan"* (New York, 1900), p. 3.

It would be easy enough at this late date simply to ignore early commentaries such as these (a recent study, for example, announces its intention to deal with Kipling "as if no revival of his reputation were in fact necessary"[9]), allowing them to fall of their own weight, to be discredited by their own extravagance and extra-literary bias, were it not for the fact that critical statements remarkably like these both in tone and substance have persistently been made all during the last three-quarters of a century and continue to be made today. Such familiar attacks, constantly reinforced as they are by apologies like Shapiro's, Hemingway's, and Pound's, cannot be lightly dismissed. Indeed, their persistence constitutes one of the cruxes of Kipling criticism, and they must therefore be faced squarely, even at the risk of alienating readers already committed to the author beyond any need for re-evaluation or excuse. For the fact is that there is a great potential Kipling readership for whom any discussion of the works must begin with at least an acknowledgment of the traditional criticisms of the author, and of these criticisms, none is more basic than the inevitable association, already alluded to, of the writer's art with his politics.

I have suggested that when people apologize for quoting from Kipling's poems and stories, what they are really trying to do is to dissociate themselves from his political attitudes, but perhaps this is just another way of saying that most Kipling readers have great difficulty distinguishing between the author's politics and his art. We know that many other writers have expressed unpopular political opinions without those opinions being seriously held against them in discussions of their work; in evaluating Lawrence or Eliot, for example, most commentators seem able to separate the writers' aesthetics from their personal

---

9. Louis Cornell, *Kipling in India* (London, 1967), p. xi.

B

politics, or at least make an effort to do so. Kipling, however, is constantly being attacked for his political views by
critics who seem to believe those views to be, for this writer
more than for most others, inextricably interwoven with
his aesthetics, and who plainly deplore that intimate relationship. When Lionel Trilling says of Kipling's "toryism"
that it often had in it "a lower-middle-class snarl of defeated gentility,"[10] he is not only attacking what seems to
him to be a reprehensible attitude, he is also, and just as
importantly, criticizing the voice—the aesthetic tone—in
which that attitude is expressed, criticizing what looks to
him like the confusion of art and "ideas" in Kipling's work,
a confusion which for Trilling amounts to the failure of
art.   Even T. S. Eliot, in his well-known appreciation of
Kipling as a writer of great "verse," cannot avoid a note of
condescension, directed in particular at this troublesome
tone. Verse, the reader may well conclude after finishing
Eliot's essay,[11] even the best verse, is, after all, not poetry.
Its special virtue is its crude, lower-class vigor, and so
whatever its other qualities, which may be considerable,
it is itself seldom purely aesthetic and therefore always has
the potential for serving other (generally political) ends.[12]

It would surely be a mistake to try to defend Kipling
against this sort of judgment by suggesting that there is in
fact *no* significant relationship in his work between politics
and art. Eight decades of readers have not been wrong to

<hr>

10. Lionel Trilling, "Kipling," *The Liberal Imagination* (New York,
1950), p. 125.

11. T. S. Eliot, "Introduction," *A Choice of Kipling's Verse* (1941;
rpt. New York, 1964).

12. And is also, therefore, forever *declassé*. The question of the extent to which the distinctions commonly made between Kipling and his
fellow artists are class distinctions would be worth exploring. Trilling's
remark is certainly suggestive in this connection, as are the Beerbohm
caricatures. In chapter five of the present study, I allude to the matter
again briefly.

see such a relationship. They may well have been very
wrong, however, to deplore it. For it is my belief that the
way to deal with Kipling is not to attempt to separate his
politics from his aesthetics in the hope—if one is an admirer
—of being left with a residue, however small, of pure art,
or—if one is a detractor—of being able to show how much
politics there is compared to art. On the contrary, the way
to deal with Kipling is to insist on the absolute relevance
of the politics to the art, of the art to the politics; to insist,
that is, that the writer who, at one point in his career,
thanked the gods for having given him "the two separate
sides of [his] head,"[13] still had, after all, a single head.

Kipling's detractors (and friends), in encouraging the
fragmentation of the artist's work, have encouraged as
well precisely that proliferation of voices which so many
readers have criticized: "the voice of a dying hierarchy,"
"a lower-middle-class snarl," "the voice of the hooligan."
What has, as a result, been lost among all of Kipling's
"voices," is Kipling's "voice," a voice which, though certainly complex and at times even self-contradictory, is
aesthetically satisfying because essentially whole and in
the deepest sense consistent. It is specifically my point in
this study that the political Kipling disliked by so many
and the artistic Kipling praised by a few are not two different Kiplings but one and the same; that the apparently
extra-literary preoccupations (imperialism, brutality, and
so on) which have always been used to explain Kipling's
failure as an artist are just the elements from which, *as an
artist*, he drew his greatest strength; in short, that for what
Ernest Hemingway called "the good Kipling," politics
were always of the very essence of aesthetics.

One of the great problems of Kipling criticism is to find
a way to discover and reveal this coherent voice of "the

---

13. See Kipling's poem "The Two-Sided Man."

good Kipling," a way to explain, that is, how Kipling the brutal realist can *simultaneously* be Kipling the man of compassion, how Kipling the mournful nihilist can *simultaneously* be Kipling the winner of the Nobel Prize for his "idealistic tendency," how Kipling the romantic imperialist and believer in order can *simultaneously* be Kipling the late-Victorian doubter, how Kipling the political man can *simultaneously* be Kipling the artist. The obvious way to discover "the good Kipling," who differs from "the bad Kipling" not in the superiority of his ideas but in the superiority of the art embodying those ideas, in his superior ability to synthesize apparently disparate elements into a satisfying aesthetic experience, is, of course, through study of his works. The moment we undertake such a project, however, we once more run up against the fact of the author's extraordinary quotability. For so dazzling and so apt are the many well-known phrases Kipling has contributed to the language, and so readily adaptable are they to political sloganeering, that it is a simple enough matter for readers to mistake the part for the whole, to suppose the idea expressed in a particular quotation to be the same as the one expressed in the coherent work from which the quotation comes.

The famous statement, for example, that "East is East, and West is West, and never the twain shall meet," is a remarkably stiff-backed, doctrinaire declaration which, perhaps for that very reason, appears almost daily somewhere in the world in a newspaper editorial or political address and which passes everywhere for one of Kipling's best known and most characteristic utterances. The fact that the third and fourth lines of the poem

But there is neither East nor West, Border, nor Breed, nor Birth,
When two strong men stand face to face, though they come
   from the ends of the earth!

clearly mitigate the absolutism and inflexibility of the first is not so well known simply because the later lines lack the brilliance of the first and so are rarely quoted. Indeed, it turns out that Kipling is considerably less inflexible in this matter than, for example, E. M. Forster, whose pessimistic conclusion to *A Passage to India* has never seemed, even to liberal readers, to require apology. We must resist the lure of Kipling's quotability, then, if for no other reason than that criticism by quotation does a disservice to a serious piece of art, makes it impossible for us to hear in it its author's true voice, implies that a writer's intuitions lie on the surfaces of his poems and stories, caught in a memorable line or two, when in fact they much more often lurk mysteriously—"fabulously," to use Bonamy Dobrée's term[14] —at an almost irrecoverable center, a center that will only yield, if it yields at all, to careful readings of whole works.

But this suggests an obvious method for discovering what, if anything, Rudyard Kipling's voice has to say today, more than a century after the author's birth, to readers who feel obliged to apologize even for mentioning his name. One major problem of Kipling criticism is, as we have seen, that an essentially political judgment of an aesthetic issue having gained almost universal acceptance, it has tended to perpetuate itself by discouraging, among serious readers, the sort of close consideration of texts upon which any literary judgment must be based. If today, therefore, we would not so much refute as move beyond this conventional judgment of Kipling, we must begin by looking carefully at whole texts in order to determine, through study of their rhythms and structures—the author's authentic voice—what they have to say as works of art.

The present study seeks to do just this and is shaped by

---

14. Bonamy Dobrée, *Rudyard Kipling; Realist and Fabulist* (London, 1967).

its intention. That is, it attempts, through extended analyses of a relatively small group of short stories, to establish the seriousness of Kipling as a literary artist and the intimate relationship in his best work between socio-political ideas and art. To readers who may have come to this book in the hope of finding a general discussion of Kipling's work, I will explain that a commitment to extended textual analysis as a method for discovering what a writer is trying to say necessarily precludes the encyclopedic approach of such fine Kipling commentaries as J. M. S. Tompkins' *The Art of Rudyard Kipling* and Bonamy Dobrée's *Rudyard Kipling: Realist and Fabulist*. These books are highly recommended to readers who want an overview. My commitment to extended textual analysis also directs my attention in this study toward Kipling's short stories, with their rich textures and complex forms, and away from his poems, brilliantly mnemonic but for the most part structurally simpler and less resonant than the stories. The focus of the study, then, is, by design, a sharp one. The object of these chapters will be to demonstrate the close relationship between "extra-literary" ideas and aesthetics in Kipling's best art, and my selection of the stories to be dealt with has been made not in the hope of denying the existence of "the bad Kipling" (whose "badness" consists of his failure to establish such a relationship), nor to stack the cards in favor of some idiosyncratic view of the writer, but simply on the principle that an artist should always be defined by his best work. And the fact is that while these discussions will concentrate on a limited number of the author's short stories, if they succeed in what they set out to do, their lessons may have a wider application.

One result of these analyses, for example, may well be the discovery of a Kipling who has survived the late nineteenth century—which provided him with so much of his vocabulary and so many of his familiar gestures—in a way which permits him to speak directly and freshly to readers today. Kipling lived through years of change and cataclysm and had the same opportunity his contemporaries did to guess the meaning of the events around him. He is not, on the basis of his political opinions, commonly credited with having guessed well, but close studies of his works may change that idea. In one of the more cryptic passages in *The Cantos*, Ezra Pound sets down the three words "Kipling suspected it."[15] Even here, it may be noted, Pound must have his touch of condescension; Kipling is not permitted to "know," only to "suspect." Nevertheless, what Kipling may merely have suspected in his own time, we can with greater certainty know today, in no small measure because of some of those works of his which we are going to examine now.

---

15. Ezra Pound, "Canto 82."

CHAPTER TWO ▨

The Law of Nature,
The Law of Art

i

To begin with, it would be useful to have a demonstration
of the way in which issues which have long been looked
upon as political by Kipling's critics really do resolve themselves, when properly examined, into matters of aesthetics.
It is the contention of this study that they do so, and, moreover, that the recognition that they do so can lead to the
solution of long-standing and stubborn critical problems.
In the poem "Recessional,"[1] for example, there occurs a
line—called, by Roger Lancelyn Green, Kipling's most notorious line—which has been troubling readers with its political and sociological overtones ever since it first appeared
more than seventy years ago, but which raises aesthetic
questions which are in a way of considerably more interest than the political. In the context of the poem the "notorious" line reads:

> If, drunk with sight of power, we loose
>   Wild tongues that have not Thee in awe,
> Such boasting as the Gentiles use
>   *Or lesser breeds without the Law*—

---

1. I have chosen this poem to deal with here because the offending
line is so well known. Discussion of one of the author's unsuccessful
stories could have made the same point, only perhaps not so tellingly.

> Lord God of Hosts, be with us yet,
> Lest we forget—lest we forget!

From the first, readers were outraged by the line which has here been italicized, offended in particular by the contempt for dark-skinned natives which appears to be implicit in the phrase "lesser breeds." Indeed, so persistently have critics been repelled by the phrase that forty-five years after the initial publication of the line, George Orwell was still able to write of it:

It is always good for a snigger in pansy-left circles. It is assumed as a matter of course that the "lesser breeds" are "natives," and a mental picture is called up of some *pukka sahib* in a pith helmet kicking a coolie.[2]

Orwell would, of course, have been the last man in the world to defend Kipling in this situation had he not felt that "in its context the sense of the line is almost the exact opposite of this,"[3] but, significantly, such an assurance has gone no further toward changing people's minds about the meaning of the line than have the many ingenious explanations offered by other Kipling authorities over the years. C. E. Carrington, for example, has written that

the distinction between those who are "within" and "without the Law" is the distinction between the men of any class or creed who are humble because they submit to the Law and those who are arrogant because they over-ride it. By their words and deeds you might know them, not by their accents or the color of their skins.[4]

And quite recently Carrington has returned to the defense of the passage, urging readers to

---

2. "Rudyard Kipling," *Essays* (New York, 1954), p. 124.
3. *Essays*, p. 124.
4. *The Life of Rudyard Kipling* (New York, 1955), p. 207.

let [the lines] speak for themselves. The form and the syntax
allow no interpretation but that this is a warning to British
imperialists against boastful arrogance, which would lower
them to the level of those other unworthy imperialists, "the
Gentiles," who are "lesser" because they are "without the Law."
Did he mean the Germans? Or the Americans? Who can say?
But to suggest that he meant the colonial peoples makes nonsense of the whole passage.[5]

Yet though critics and scholars have continued to offer
their interpretations and reinterpretations over the last
three decades, the old reading of the line still persists. On
May 8th, 1964, *Time* magazine reported that

last week delegates approved the first new Methodist hymnal
in 29 years. The song book drops some familiar samples of 19th
century hymnody, such as Rudyard Kipling's "Recessional,"
which Negro Methodists claim has an unmistakable racial slur
in its reference to "lesser breeds without the Law."[6]

And even those critics who have accepted Orwell's explanation that " 'lesser breeds' refers almost certainly to the
Germans,"[7] have been reluctant to give up their feelings
about the phrase. "It may be a relief," John Gross writes,
for example, in the *New Statesman*, "to learn that the lesser
breeds without the Law were meant to be, not Africans or
Asians, but the rulers of Wilhelmine Germany—but why
bring in breeds, anyway?"[8]

Gross here puts the whole matter very neatly into focus.
Not even the most ingenious explanations, he seems to be
saying, can legitimize a line of poetry that *sounds* wrong,

---

5. "Lesser Breeds Without the Law," letter to *Times Literary Sup-
plement* (4 May 1967), 379.

6. P. 75.

7. *Essays*, p. 124.

8. "Black Thoughts from Abroad," *New Statesman* (12 June 1964),
913.

and in making this point, he does more to honor Kipling as an artist than do all the friendly critics with their elaborate interpretations of the passage. For what Kipling's friends imply, with their painstaking research and their paraphrasing, is that the author is essentially a political personage, one who, in a policy statement entitled "Recessional," has been inappropriately frank, but who can be saved from the consequences of his unfortunate lapse by a simple redefinition of terms and an appeal to historical precedent. Significantly, the poem itself from which the line comes is entirely ignored in these commentaries, except where its manifest content, the "statement" which it makes in so many words, can be used to support the position of the defenders. As an organic work of art, however, it never enters the discussion. The question is "what does the line mean?" and not "is 'Recessional' a good poem?" What Gross's statement does, however, is to raise just this question of aesthetics. For by announcing that, in spite of all the explanations, the line still refuses to resonate properly for him—"why bring in breeds, anyway?"—he forces us to deal, at least for the moment, with the line's "sound" rather than with its sense, forces us to listen to the tonality of Kipling's voice (by which I mean the effect which the poem as a whole creates) rather than to the excerptable ideas the poet is expressing; forces us, in short, to consider "Recessional" as a work of art rather than as a political document.

"Recessional" has nearly always been treated politically and/or historically. The event which occasioned the publication of the poem was, of course, historically significant. In 1897, England was celebrating Victoria's Jubilee, and artists of all sorts vied with one another to see who could produce the most extravagant praise of Queen and Country. In the midst of this patriotic spectacle, the celebrants waited in considerable suspense for the voice that, during the previous half-dozen years, had come to be associated with—had become almost synonymous with—Britain's imperial destiny; and it was perhaps just this expectation which made Kipling's words so shocking when they did come. On July 17, 1897, "Recessional" appeared in the *London Times* (having been rescued at the last moment, according to one story, from a waste basket).[9] The title itself must have struck the first readers as unusual, suggesting, as it does, not triumph and glory, but rather withdrawal, waning, a going-away. And the rest of the poem, with its clear references to the impermanence of power and to the need for humility in an uncertain world, surprised Kipling's countrymen, revealing to them, in C. E. Carrington's adulatory prose, "their heartfelt but unrealized emotion. Humility not pride, awe not arrogance, a sense of transience not a sense of permanence were to be the keynotes of the imperial festival. Again, Kipling confounded the critics by revealing an aspect of his genius which many of them grudged him."[10]

The first thing to be noted is that everything Carrington has to say about the actual content of the poem is quite correct. The explicit subject of "Recessional," as the title implies, is indeed the impermanence of power and the need for humility. Yet for all this, the poem strikes readers like Gross as an extraordinarily arrogant one. How is such a contradiction possible? Evidently, because a poem does not express the specific ideas contained in its words and phrases nearly so much as it expresses *itself*, its own structure and wholeness, or lack of it. "Recessional" has an obvious structure and an equally obvious lack of wholeness, and at every moment these qualities work against the mani-

---

9.   Carrington, p. 206.
10.   Carrington, p. 206.

fest content of the poem to communicate an idea very different from the work's nominal one.

The form, or more particularly the sound, of "Recessional" creates the first disparity. Kipling tells us that he wrote the poem to the tune of the hymn "Eternal Father, Strong to Save,"[11] a typically four-square Church piece whose regular tread and comfortingly familiar cadences have left their mark on the poem, inevitably suggesting not the transience of power and the need for humility, but rather the security and self-congratulatory clubbiness of a not-very-demanding religion. Beyond this, the poem repeatedly implies values which directly contradict those it explicitly endorses. "Beneath whose awful hand we hold/ Dominion over palm and pine . . ." suggests, for example, some sort of supernal ratification of Britain's imperial destiny which ill-assorts with the poem's announced theme of humility; while the fourth stanza, quoted above and containing the passage about "lesser breeds," seems to urge England to be contrite principally on the grounds that the chosen of God ought to be more scrupulous than anyone else.

It is this discrepancy between the announced and the implicit subject of the poem, then—what we have called the lack of wholeness—which makes the specific line about "lesser breeds" so offensive. It is of no real importance what race or nationality is identified with the word "breeds"; all such efforts at identification are in the long run a waste of time. What is dismaying about the line is its inherent act of "presuming to judge" in the context of a poem whose ostensible subject is the arrogance of such judgments. Thus, the failure of "Recessional" is aesthetic not political, and thus "lesser breeds without the Law" fails as a line of

---

11. Carrington, p. 204.

poetry much more importantly than it does as a political utterance.

None of this discussion is intended to suggest that concern for the meaning of the line is irrelevant. Readers are quite right to wonder whether in order to read Kipling at all they may not first be obliged to accept as givens certain distasteful political attitudes. For the author has always been represented as an artist who demands such prior commitments from his readers. But this gets to the very heart of the relationship between ideas and aesthetics in art. The greatest artist may be defined (in this context) as the one who demands the fewest prior commitments to ideas from his readers; may be defined, that is, as the one who is most successful at creating a world all of whose ideas proceed plausibly and convincingly from the inner necessity of that world. We have suggested that a poem like "Recessional" fails because instead of being a coherent organism, expressing its own unique vision in its own inevitable voice, it is—to quote a phrase Kipling used on another occasion— "a thing imposed from without,"[12] a work which, because it lacks structural integrity, seeks to exploit certain sources of energy external to itself—pre-existing attitudes toward the propriety of Britain's imperial role, for instance—to which it has not earned the right. Readers are making an aesthetic judgment, then, when they say that they will not read Kipling because they don't approve of his ideas; what they really mean is that they will not read him because he has failed to create a world in which those ideas exist necessarily and plausibly, apart from the reader's approval or disapproval of them. In short, what they are saying is that Kipling is not really an artist.

But the question of whether or not Kipling is an artist is

---

12. Rudyard Kipling, *Something of Myself* (New York, 1937), p. 228.

just the one we have undertaken to consider in this study. Nor will our concentration on the form and structure of Kipling's works mean that we will have to ignore the traditional questions about the author's politics. For if politics and aesthetics are as intimately associated in Kipling's works as has been suggested here, then a discussion of stories and poems as works of art will inevitably return us to the familiar political issues. The difference might well be, however, that where we find a work of art that is aesthetically satisfying—one which is, in other words, a product of "the good Kipling"—we may also find such matters as the relationship between white men and black, and the confrontation of the individual and the Law—both matters suggested by the line about "lesser breeds"—expressed with an inevitability that removes them from the realm of political criticism.

ii

A good story to investigate in this connection would be "Without Benefit of Clergy." Though the story has frequently been praised as one of Kipling's finest—indeed, as "one of the best short stories of all time"[13]—like most of Kipling's work it has received comparatively little close critical attention. Perhaps because so many of Kipling's stories are so (apparently, at least) accessible, so universally appealing, they have never seemed to demand the sort of serious attention critics naturally devote to the short fiction of Joyce or Lawrence or Faulkner. One reader, for example, has said of "Without Benefit of Clergy" that it does not require interpretation but "needs only to be dis-

---

13. F. T. Cooper, *Some English Story-Tellers* (New York, 1912), p. 142. See also W. Somerset Maugham, "Introduction," *Maugham's Choice of Kipling's Best* (New York, 1953), p. xx.

played,"[14] yet no Kipling story more richly repays close reading than this early tale of the marriage of a British colonial official and an Indian girl and their efforts to survive in a fortuitous universe.

As it is pictured in "Without Benefit of Clergy," that universe is blundering, directionless, and very nearly incapable of supporting human life. If it operates at all on any rational principles, these principles are concealed from man, who, in his remote corner of the cosmos, is always trying to discover some Law inherent in things upon which to model his own life, but who sees instead only meaningless, random violence and the constant threat of accidental annihilation. Holden's thoughts, in the course of the story, are constantly filled with visions of death; his sensations are at one point described as those of a man who has attended his own funeral. It is through Holden, through his experiences and his persistent premonitions, that we come to sense the precariousness of life. When Ameera is about to give birth and Holden must leave her for two weeks, he writes out in his own hand a wire announcing her death, deposits it with a servant, and then spends each day grimly awaiting its arrival. Later, when cholera has broken out, the two lovers "kiss each other and shiver," and Holden hesitates about going to his office, thinking that "there were twelve hours in each day when he could not see Ameera, and she might die in three. He was absolutely certain that her death would be demanded." Holden's colleagues collapse overnight and are replaced before they can be missed, only a laconic telegram recording the fact that they ever existed. "Ricketts, Myndonie. Dying. Holden relieve. Immediate."

This threat of disaster broods over the whole story, and

14. J. M. S. Tompkins, *The Art of Rudyard Kipling* (London, 1959), p. 118.

the sense of the irrationality of life is always lurking in the background. The people of India wait dully for the rains that do not come and that no action of theirs can bring. They watch hopelessly as the drought "turns the earth to iron" and brings with it the promise of death, a death that is doubly terrible because it is as cheap as life and no more significant. Under the "red and heavy audit" all men are helpless. "The land was very sick and needed a little breathing-space ere the torrent of cheap life could flood it anew. The children of immature fathers and undeveloped mothers made no resistance. They were cowed and sat still, waiting till the sword should be sheathed in November if it were so willed." The end of the terror, it appears, will be no less accidental, no more meaningful, than its beginning.

This grim picture of a universe indifferent or inimical to man turns up regularly in Kipling's fiction, frequently as the main theme. In "Mrs. Bathurst," for example, the discovery, by Pritchard and the others, of the indifference of the universe is the central business of the story. In "Without Benefit of Clergy," however, the emphasis is not so much on the fact of the irrationality of things as it is on people's reactions to that irrationality. Life's essential insanity is taken pretty much for granted by the people who live in the plague-ridden corner of India in which the story is set. These people are resigned to death's being sudden and violent and unreasonable. Their resignation, however, does not reduce their need for reassurance and peace, their need to find a Law by which to guide their lives. If anything, it intensifies that need and sends them off in search of spiritual comfort. And Kipling follows them in their search, examining the conventions, the codes and the rituals which they have developed to ease the burden of life's uncertainty.

The rituals of the two worlds have more in common than

c

may at first appear. True, the native ceremonies are based largely on superstition, while the British customs seem more scientifically or psychologically defensible. The classic English insistence, for example, on "dressing for dinner in the jungle," performs the real function of maintaining inner discipline and a sense of order. And, of course, sending wives and children up to the cool hills for the Indian hot weather is, medically speaking, a sensible thing to do. Yet a reader of "Without Benefit of Clergy" very soon comes to sense that the appeal of such acts as these, and of others like them, is far more ceremonial than rational; that it is not so much the scientific basis of these customs as the almost mystical pleasure and comfort their repetition gives which accounts for their persistence. Ask a British clubman the reason for some long-established prohibition, and his response is likely to be not an explanation—which may, in fact, exist—but rather a flat statement of faith: "It simply is not done." And it is in this crucial way that English and native ceremonies are so similar. They both fulfill a need for reassurance that has been created by the uncertainty and the hostility of the environment; they both make their appeals primarily to the central core of fear in human beings that will not yield to reason, and which, in India at any rate, has so much to thrive on.

There are many such British customs and rituals described in detail in "Without Benefit of Clergy." Most of them center around the club which the English have set up in their compound. In the club, carefully patterned after comparable establishments at home, the rules are quite elaborate and are very strictly enforced, the more so for being, sometimes, ludicrously inappropriate. When Holden returns to his station, for example, after two weeks of duty in the field, the last thing in the world he wants to do is to visit the club. Having left Ameera two weeks before when she was on the point of giving birth—a precarious business at best in those days and in that place—he now longs to hurry to his house in the city. Yet his first act, on returning to the compound, is to spend two hours eating dinner at the club. He is miserable, he chafes at the restriction, but apparently it never occurs to him to skip this ritual meal altogether. He knows that so shocking and enormous a breach of protocol must inevitably endanger the secret of his life with Ameera. Indeed, the very secrecy of that life further testifies to the power of convention. The British, who stand ready at any hour to give their lives for the Indian people, nevertheless balk at accepting them as equals, and drive men like Holden into the pointless subterfuges of a double life.

Holden's acceptance of the club, however, is not simply politic. He genuinely needs what that establishment has to offer, as the other men in the station do. He needs the billiard tables and the shop talk. His love for his Indian wife is real, but the call of the old life is equally real. Ameera knows this and always speaks of the time when her husband, and even her son, will return to their own people. Holden, leaving his wife's bedside and tremendously agitated after the first glimpse of his child, knows quite instinctively where to turn for relief. " 'I never felt like this in my life,' he thought. 'I'll go to the club and pull myself together.' " That last phrase is an especially apt one. Indeed, the key to all the English conventions which Kipling enumerates in "Without Benefit of Clergy," and which are so important to an understanding of the story, is self-control, a pulling of oneself together, that tradition of reticence which, perhaps quite automatic in Britain, must, in a place like India, be artificially kept up. For life in India may best be described as blatant. People eke out their precarious existences literally in the streets, and death usually fails to observe the amenities. It is not suprising, then, that men for whom understatement is a way of life feel uneasy in such a lurid world and need conventions to help them face it. In the club, self-control is easier to achieve; the most terrible news of life and death may be communicated dispassionately. "It was the Deputy Commissioner of Kot-Kumharsen, staying at the club for a day, who lightly told a tale that made Holden's blood run cold as he overheard the end." Holden, nervous even in the club about his wife and child, asks anxiously, but even so a little off-handedly, "Is it the old programme then . . . famine, fever, and cholera?" To which the Deputy Commissioner replies with the expected irony, "Oh no. Only local scarcity and an unusual prevalence of seasonal sickness. You'll find it all in the reports if you live till next year."

Compared to the reticent and quasi-rational conventions of the British, the native rites seem almost flamboyantly mystical. "Without Benefit of Clergy" opens on just such a note of extravagance, with Holden saying "But if it be a girl?" and Ameera replying "Lord of my life, it cannot be. I have prayed for so many nights, and sent gifts to Sheikh Bal's shrine so often, that I know God will give us a son—a manchild that shall grow into a man." A few lines later the girl continues in the same vein. "The mullah of the Patten mosque shall cast his nativity—God send he be born in an auspicious hour!" Kipling is here establishing, in the very first lines of his story, the theme of ritual as a hedge against disaster. But these lines only begin to introduce the subject. As we read on we soon see that the story contains many such references. The drama is played out, for example, against the background of a teeming Indian city, crowded with millions of the faithful, who live in the shadows of the mosques and minarets and whose only defense against the terrors of the unknown is a naively hopeful mixture of religion and magic. Kipling does not overdo this background material. Instead, he lets us glimpse an occasional sacred procession or hear, as if from far away, a muttered prayer rising from the city. Elsewhere, however, and notably in "The City of Dreadful Night," he describes such scenes in detail with the heat, the disease, the deaths and, floating over the huddled rooftops, the rousing, mysterious challenge of faith, the *Muezzins'* repeated calls to prayer and the answering professions of belief—"'I bear witness that there is no God but God." Indeed, these are the very words Ameera whispers into the ears of her baby when the child has been put into her arms for the first time. Though she is only half-conscious, her first impulse is to place her son under the protection of religion.

Magic plays as large a part as religion in the system of rituals which the Indian natives have developed. When, for example, Holden hurries into the room where his wife and child are lying, he steps on a naked dagger that has been placed on the threshold to avert ill-luck. "It broke at the hilt under his impatient heel. 'God is great!' cooed Ameera in the half-light. 'Thou hast taken his misfortunes on thy head.'" Later, when the baby is older, he becomes the object of all of his mother's superstitious hopes and fears. "I know a charm to make him wise as Suleiman and Aflatoun [Solomon and Plato]," Ameera says one day. "She drew from the embroidered bag a handful of almonds. 'See! I give the parrot one half and Tota the other.'" She gives a piece of almond to the child "who ate it slowly with wondering eyes. 'This I will do each day of seven, and without doubt he who is ours will be a bold speaker and wise.'"

Holden is himself a participant in what is the most fully and brilliantly reported of all the native rituals. Coming from his first sight of the child, he encounters his servant,

Pir Khan, who is waiting in the courtyard below with two goats and a sabre. When Holden asks bewilderedly what this paraphernalia is for he is told "For the birth sacrifice. What else? Otherwise the child, being unguarded from fate, may die." (Kipling's own birth was "hastened" by the sacrifice of a goat.) Holden, initiated by Ameera into some of the native customs, had long ago learned, almost as a joke, the fitting words to be said on such an occasion. Now, with a heightened sense of life's precariousness and of his new responsibility, he does not dare reject any possible protection. "Hardly knowing what he did, Holden cut twice as he muttered the Mahommedan prayer that runs: 'Almighty! In place of this my son I offer life for life, blood for blood, head for head, bone for bone, hair for hair, skin for skin.'"

Ameera, for her part, has learned many of the English rituals from Holden, since no one can say for sure who may have discovered the true charm, the unique combination of words and gestures that will infallibly placate the Powers. Thus when she prays, mere common sense dictates that she pray both to the Prophet and to Beebee Miriam [the Virgin Mary]. And later, when she has come to herself again after the death of her baby, she accepts the wisdom of British reticence in the face of jealous gods, and decides she and Holden "must make no protestations of delight, but go softly underneath the stars," lest God find them out. "It is naught, it is naught," she says after every moment of happiness, hoping that all the Powers will hear.

The Powers, however, either because they do not exist or because they fail to listen, do not hear. Indeed, what is most striking about this story is that in the world which it pictures, ritual—elaborate and hopeful and time-consuming as it is—is of no use at all. Powerless either to alter the decrees of the universe or to prepare men to accept the consequences of those decrees, it is, from beginning to end, pathetic hocus-pocus and nothing more. Pir Khan, himself devoted to ritual, sums this truth up best when he hurries to Holden with the news that Ameera has been stricken with black cholera. "When there is a cry in the night," he says, "and the spirit flutters into the throat, who has a charm that will restore?" This is just the point that is made earlier in the story when Ameera prays for "a man-child that shall grow into a man." She does have a son, of course, but in a striking illustration of the low efficiency of ritual, the boy does not live. For all her prayers, Kipling seems to be saying, Ameera is no better served by the gods than she is by the laws of chance.

In a crisis, every sort of ritual is hollow. Holden feels only frustration at the obligatory dinner given for him at the club, and the news he receives there about the cholera epidemic terrifies him as much as it does precisely because it is offered in such a ritualistically off-hand way. When he is in trouble he turns to the traditional solace of work, but work helps him little. Forced to leave Ameera just when she needs him most, he does his work so badly that the fact is noticed by all his colleagues. And when his son dies, he is not "alive to the kindness of the gods" who present him with an "unusually heavy mail that demanded concentrated attention and hard work." Even the most unfailingly restorative of rituals, eating, is useless in the face of Holden's sorrow. Ahmed Khan's curried eggs are no more helpful in assuaging grief than the knife on the threshold, the sacrifice of the goats, or the seven almonds of wisdom were in preventing it.

This failure of ritual is suggested in still other ways. During the drought and famine, for example, "the conches in the Hindu temples screamed and bellowed, for the gods were inattentive in those days." Cholera "struck a pilgrim-gathering of half a million at a sacred shrine. Many died at the feet of their god." And once, in a conversation with Holden, Ameera asks "will my prayers be heard?" Holden's answer is carelessly conventional. "God is very good," he says. To which Ameera replies, "Of that I am not sure."

iii

The failure of ritual, a fact which is central to the meaning of "Without Benefit of Clergy," is inevitable, given ritual's function—to achieve order in a chaotic world. It is true that different men conceive of this function in different ways. On the one hand, comparatively primitive people turn to ritual as a means of ordering the physical universe. They long to control the forces of life, and in their elaborate ceremonies they often seem to be presenting to the universe models of behavior in the hope that the universe will comply and shape itself a little closer to their desires. More sophisticated men, on the other hand, who have surer if less dramatic methods of dealing with nature, nevertheless persist in their own adherence to ritual, not so much because they think it will help them to organize the universe as because they hope that it will help them to establish a little order in themselves. In either case, however, the passion for order is a key to the understanding of ritual.

In this connection, there is a revealing passage early in "Without Benefit of Clergy" in which Holden, thinking seriously for the first time of the child that is to come, finds that he cannot help but feel uneasy. "And there was going to be added to this kingdom a third person whose arrival Holden felt inclined to resent. It interfered with his perfect happiness. It disarranged the orderly peace of the house that was his own." If Holden's reaction is not all that a storybook father's should be, it at least has the virtue of being honest and, in addition, of being thoroughly in character. For Holden, we must not forget, is a young man who has come out to India to do something about the sprawling sub-continent, the huge, confusing country which, with its teeming masses of people and its violence and disease, is the ultimate metaphor for chaos, just as the British administrative passion is a striking metaphor for man's desire to impose order on confusion. Thus, in his longing for order and peace in the house that is his own, Holden is only longing for what all men desire and what they often find it necessary to invent rituals and codes to achieve.

But order, seen in these terms, seems such a thoroughly respectable goal. If it is indeed order that is the object of ritual, can this same order also be the reason for ritual's failure? In "Without Benefit of Clergy," as in many other of his stories, Kipling seems to be suggesting that this is so. Not that he is sentimental about confusion and incompetence. That is the last thing in the world he can be accused of. Order obviously has its place, as the many successes of the British in India testify. There is nothing in the least edifying, for example, about the chaos of famine, and so we read with a certain satisfaction that "on the heels of the spring-reapings came a cry for bread, and the Government, which had decreed that no man should die of want, sent wheat."

Such an example of control on the political level is certainly to be applauded, and Kipling, as much as any writer, has been quick to celebrate the man of action, the bridge-builder, the engineer, the administrator. But "Without Benefit of Clergy" is not a story about politics. To be sure, in the concentric worlds which surround the little house in the city, policy is everyone's chief concern. At the club, for instance, the talk is always "beating up round the ever-fresh subject of each man's work." But such talk remains

always in the background; we hear very little of it. What
we do hear constantly in this story is the long, sometimes
interrupted but always renewed, conversation of Holden
and Ameera as the two talk together in their room or on
the roof of their house about the inexplicable way of the
world and about the inordinate difficulty of coming to
terms with it. And it is on this level, this personal level, that
ritual fails most conspicuously in the story, because, as
Kipling shows us, it is on this level that a passion for order
is most fruitless and corrupting.

Why this should be so is not difficult to see. A passionate
love of order inevitably implies a certain distaste for the
world as it is actually constituted, implies a great longing
to substitute for the disorganized reality of today, the perfectly structured artifice of tomorrow. How else explain
the Englishman's willingness to die for the India of his
plans and schemes and projects, and yet his refusal to accept the Indians, like Ameera, of the here and now? But
the cluttered and untidy reality of the present so easily dismissed by orderly men—what is it, Kipling seems to be asking, but the only reality there is? Love, however much we
may anticipate it for the future, can only be experienced
in the present, the author tries to show, and life, however
much we plan it better for tomorrow, can only be lived today. What's more, a law of compensation seems inevitably
to apply to life, decreeing that any provision made for the
future must be made at the expense of the present, so that
a man may not grow rich taking money from one pocket
and putting it into another.

Ameera, for one, is quick to recognize the operation of
this law. For much of the story she is bitter at the thought
of how Englishwomen live longer and retain their youth
and beauty longer than Indian women do. Always in her
mind is the dread that she will soon be old and ugly and

that Holden will leave her for one of the *mem-log*. Indeed, when we first meet her she is extremely self-conscious about her status, and her insistence upon defining herself in terms of the white lady seems to be one of her most important rituals. But when she learns that the white women accomplish their miracle by leaving their husbands for the six months of the hot weather and by turning their children over to nurses, her envy turns to contempt, her ritual longing for status vanishes the way all her other rituals vanish in the course of the story.

The activities of the *mem-log* astound as much as they disgust her. Why, she wonders, should a woman want to live long and be beautiful except for the love of her husband and children? And if this is so, what madness possesses her to give up both husband and children in order to prolong that life and beauty? What end can she hope to achieve by postponing the experience of love from today until tomorrow, especially in a random and irrational universe in which the chance is always great that there will be no tomorrow? From a purely practical point of view Ameera's own refusal to withdraw to the hills may seem foolishly willful. But in the sense that it represents her passionate commitment to an idea, to the idea that life—infinitely precious and, from all she has seen of it, extremely tenuous—is meaningful only when it is being lived, that same refusal is shown to be courageous and honest. Thus Ameera does not, as one critic has suggested, eat herself up in the process of envying the white woman. Her decision to remain behind in the plains with Holden is based not on embarrassment or fear but on love.

"Without Benefit of Clergy" contains other characters who, like the *mem-log*, have abandoned the reality of human love to pursue an ephemeral and empty security. Ameera's old mother is one, her key to order and control being the acquisition of money and possessions. Having early been left penniless, she solved her problem by selling Ameera to Holden and would, we are told, have sold her "shrieking to the Prince of Darkness if the price had been sufficient." Her reaction to her daughter's death is especially in character. The girl has hardly breathed her last when the old woman is at Holden, tormenting him unmercifully about the few sticks of furniture she hopes to inherit. "In her anxiety to take stock of the house fittings," Kipling tells us, "she forgot to mourn."

The English administrators at their clubs also suffer from a mistrust of life which shows up in an exaggerated concern for order and propriety. Their reticence and their insularity are only ritualistic ways of postponing or avoiding human experience. Involved as they are in their work, they are shown to be too preoccupied with the horrors of tomorrow to react today, too busy constructing safe imitations of their old life to appreciate, as Holden does, the reality that is all around them. For as Holden would be the first to admit, the disruption of his orderly home is a small price to pay for his son. Such reality, he has learned, is always to be preferred to artifice, and reassuring Ameera one evening, for the thousandth time, that he will never abandon her for one of the *mem-log*, he says "I have seen fire-balloons by the hundred. I have seen the moon, and—then I saw no more fire-balloons."

Ritual, then, Kipling suggests, involves the sacrifice of what a man actually has for what he thinks he would prefer, and it is the writer's purpose in "Without Benefit of Clergy" to expose the fraud of such a sacrifice, to show how, in attempting to comfort and reassure us, it involves us instead in the tautology of giving up the very life we may be trying to achieve. "Strike!" says Pir Khan to Holden, as the Englishman is about to sacrifice the two goats. "Never life came into the world but life was paid for it." To which Holden replies with the words of the prayer, offering "life for life, blood for blood, head for head, bone for bone, hair for hair, skin for skin." But nothing can be gained, Kipling points out, from bargains like this, for it is not a man's business to haggle with the universe (using his life as the medium of exchange), no matter what formal name he may give to that haggling. It is a man's business, rather, to live as fully as he can, postponing nothing, recognizing in advance that the more he has, the more he is likely to lose, but not sacrificing any part of experience in the hope of being able to find a happiness he will not have to pay for. This is the "Law" that Holden and Ameera discover in "Without Benefit of Clergy" and which becomes the story's theme.

In order to express such a theme within the framework of a piece of fiction, Kipling has dramatically set two forces against one another. On one side there is a world full of fear and of rituals to drive out fear: there is India, burdened with death and with terror of the unknown, turning to religion and magic in an effort to find meaning and order in the universe; there are the English with their conventions and forms, anxious to serve but too quick, in the name of self-sacrifice, to postpone living to a more auspicious time. On the other side, there is the secret household in the city, there is Holden with his refreshing desire to move beyond the narrow official experiences of his peers, and there is Ameera.

Though some readers have tended to think of Ameera as mysterious and elusive, an exotic oriental beauty whose "story is removed from reality and the judgments of reality,"[15] her experiences are in fact elemental and universal

---

15. Walter M. Hart, *Kipling the Story-Writer* (Berkeley, 1918), p. 70.

and are presented with an extraordinary faithfulness to everyday detail. Moreover, her reactions to these experiences are absolutely honest; there is not a trace of the sentimentalist in her. It would be a great mistake, for example, to think that because she addresses her husband in certain conventionally exaggerated terms of self-abasement, her relationship to him is in any sense that of a slave to a master.[16] On the contrary, the marriage of Ameera and Holden, as Kipling depicts it, is founded on mutual respect and on honesty, with Ameera, if a choice must be made, even more realistic than her husband. Holden is occasionally guilty of trying to humor his wife, of turning her questions aside, as we have seen, with conventional answers. But Ameera never permits such tactics and never practices them herself. She is no Madame Butterfly, building her life on self-deception. When Holden tries to pretend that the money he paid her mother was a dowry, Ameera instantly replies, "What talk is yours of dower! I was bought as though I had been a Lucknow dancing-girl instead of a child." And when Holden goes on to ask "Art thou sorry for the sale?" Ameera does not immediately give the easy

---

16.   Hart's conclusion about the story may well have been influenced by the style of the conversations between Holden and Ameera. In Edmund Wilson's words (*The Wound and the Bow*, p. 117), Kipling has his characters "talk an English which translates their own idiom," and it is this speech—full of "thee" and "thou," "my King" and "my Queen"—which has no doubt misled certain critics into reading the story as a quaint, rather sentimental love idyll. This technique, not the same at all as dialect, of course, does, on occasion, help the author to create a heightened and poetic effect, but not one of unreality. With an almost imperceptible adjustment of vision, the reader can see these lines not as passages of stilted, sentimental prose, but as translations into English of expressions which, in the original, are completely idiomatic and unselfconscious. Indeed, Kipling several times tries to help his readers make this adjustment, often by quite plainly calling their attention to the fact that he is translating. At one point he explains a line which in English seems to have little meaning by indicating that the passage involves a pun in the original.

answer. "I have sorrowed," she says. Considering all this, it is hard to accept the notion that Ameera is "entirely ignorant," and that she "is executed by the gods in her ignorance."[17] Ameera seems, in fact, to be the shrewdest person in "Without Benefit of Clergy," and on her deathbed, especially, she is portrayed as having achieved an insight into reality, into the law of things-as-they-are, which cannot be founded on ignorance.

She was not, of course, born with this knowledge. At the age of sixteen she brought to a precipitate marriage all the strange notions, old wives' tales, magical charms and tag ends of dubious advice that a person must make do with in the world before he has acquired some experience of his own. In her addiction to rituals and conventions she is no different from anyone else in the story. Even Holden, with his ability to break away from the rigid formulae of British caste and with his painful insight into the precariousness of the world, seems sometimes to have an almost mystical faith in the ability of his wooden gate, guarded by Pir Khan, to keep out the sorrow and danger of life. Sorrow comes to all men, of course, but has the effect of confirming most of them in the wisdom of their retreat behind the wooden gates of ritual and ceremony. What is so remarkable about Ameera is that each blow that life inflicts on her makes her not more and more a prisoner of the superstitions she started with, but somehow more and more free of them. With the death of the little boy, for example, the magic charms vanish from the story and do not return. In their place there appears temporarily a certain wariness of life. "It was because we loved Tota that he died. The jealousy of God was upon us," Ameera says. "We must make no protestation of delight, but go softly underneath the stars, lest God find us out."

---

17. Tompkins, p. 101.

But such a ritual does not satisfy her for long, either. It is plainly self-defeating, requiring that she live less in order to live more, deny love in order to preserve it. As she recovers slowly from Tota's death, she senses that a deeper love has grown up between Holden and herself, and this leads her to understand the real meaning of her experience. She understands, that is, that sorrow is not the ultimate disaster of life, to be avoided at all costs, even at the expense of life itself, but rather that it is the natural complement of joy beyond which it is sometimes possible to pass to a joy even more intense. Once she recognizes this fact, she is free of the drag of ritual with its useless self-sacrifice, free to live without fear.

The last months of her life are successful in a new way. "There are not many happinesses," Kipling writes, summing up the theme of his story, "so complete as those that are snatched under the shadow of the sword. . . . They sat together and laughed, calling each other openly by every pet name that could move the wrath of the gods." When death comes at last, it is merely another random accident, without moral significance. Holden might just as easily have died in Ameera's place, or they both might just as easily have survived. Ameera is in a coma when Holden reaches her bedside, but as the first drops of rain begin to fall on the roof and as shouts of joy rise from the parched city at the return of life, she rallies. Holden stoops lower, and Ameera forms her last words on his ear, just as a few years earlier she had formed on her baby's ear the words of the profession of faith—"I bear witness that there is no God but God." Only now the words have been slightly but significantly changed to a profession of a new faith. "I bear witness," she says, "I bear witness—that there is no God but— thee, beloved!"

Coming from a woman as honest and as proud as

Ameera, this statement is clearly no sentimental hyperbole. Rather, it represents a courageous decision on the girl's part, at the moment of her death, to abandon the comfort of the old religion[18] and to substitute for the ritual of her fathers an affirmation of the Law she has learned in her life. For the love she has experienced, Ameera knows and Kipling has skillfully shown us, is for her the one reality in the world. Everything else, as J. M. S. Tompkins has suggested, is ranged in concentric tiers around that experience and grows more and more illusory the further it moves from the center. In the first circle lies the world of Holden's job, the paper work and the conventional social relationships. Beyond that, and still dimmer, is England, barely an influence, understanding nothing, represented by the ridiculous figure of the Member for Lower Tooting who is so ignorant that he singles out for his special approval the very flowers which foretell the disaster that is to come. And beyond everything there is the universe which, though it may randomly impose suffering and death, is nevertheless most unreal of all. What Ameera affirms at her death, then, is that life is lived best when it is lived without fear or hesitation, without surrender to ritual—in short, when it is lived without benefit of clergy.

Kipling's titles are often ambiguous, providing clues to the meanings of his stories which must be searched for diligently. This is especially the case here. Most readers

---

18. It is true that many of Ameera's actions derive from the behavior which is prescribed for one of her culture and religion. We have already commented, for example, on her language of self-abnegation, and here she seems to be expressing the standard idea that when a Moslem woman marries, her husband becomes her god. However, the profound conviction with which she makes the statement—and Ameera is characterized throughout the story as a person who will speak only what she herself accepts as the truth—indicates that she has made this belief her own and that it does indeed represent her personal, hard-won, and final vision of the universe.

D

have sensed the richness and complexity of this title, though without necessarily discovering all of its significance.[19] They have seen, for example, that on one level, it refers to the fact that Holden and Ameera were never properly married. In that sense, the phrase has a smug and priggish quality, a tone of outraged morality[20] which makes it especially ironic in the face of the exemplary marriage. That, of course, is just the point. It is the uselessness of ceremony, the theme so often reiterated in this story, which gives fullest meaning to the title. "By every rule and law," we are told, the love of Ameera and Holden should not have been possible. But rules and laws (of the wrong kind) are weak things. "It was a contract," we read, "entered into with a light heart," but despite the absence of official sanction it became the most binding contract in the lovers' lives. In the last analysis the title represents Kipling's approval of the couple, of their life together and, perhaps especially, of Ameera's courageous death.

For if it is difficult enough to live without benefit of clergy, it is even harder to die without it, to reject the reassurance that ritual can give at the moment of death. We

---

19.   See especially Miss Tompkins' analysis, p. 101, and Hart's comments, p. 69. Benefit of clergy, so-called, was technically a privilege allowed to members of the clergy under common law when they were charged with a crime. It meant that they were responsible only to their bishops or the church courts and that ordinary courts had no power over them. All clerks later were given the benefit of clergy, a clerk being defined as anyone who could read or write, and the act of reading a selected passage to prove literacy was known as "reading the neck verse." Miss Tompkins suggests that in this story Ameera is executed "in her ignorance" because she is unable, figuratively, to read her neck verse; that is, she cannot show herself to be deserving of special privilege. But the whole point of "Without Benefit of Clergy" would seem to be just the opposite of this: in the universe which Kipling depicts in the story, there are no "clergy," no one is privileged, no one, British or Indian, gets a second chance.

20.   There is a suggestion of this tone in the remark by Cyril Falls that Kipling wove his story "out of materials sordid enough." *Rudyard Kipling* (New York, 1915), p. 95.

should not underestimate the magnitude of Ameera's achievement. She dies a bitter death, knowing, and not trying to conceal from herself the knowledge, that her celebration of life, triumphant as it is, inevitably involves recognition of the nothingness that is left when life is gone. "There is *no* God but thee, beloved." Indeed, it is on this very note of utter annihilation that Kipling chooses to end his story, anxious that no reader should finish the work imagining that its final position is one of easy affirmation. Holden rushes away from his dead wife into a torrent of rain. Three days later the downpour has almost obliterated the house, and the landlord announces that he will finish the job the rains have begun.

'I will have it pulled down—the timber will sell for something always. It shall be pulled down, and the Municipality shall make a road across, as they desire, from the burning-ghat to the city wall, so that no man may say where this house stood.'

A few days more pass and all traces of the life that had been so full are gone forever.

iv

The world-vision of "Without Benefit of Clergy" is in many ways surprisingly modern—almost, indeed, existential, though one hesitates to use such a frequently overworked word. Certainly, however, Kipling seems in this work to have foreshadowed a number of twentieth-century works of fiction, not only thematically but in terms of plot structure as well. For example, when Holden hurries away through the rain at the end of the story, leaving his dead wife behind, he does not know that forty years later an even more famous fictional hero will reenact this same scene. Lieutenant Henry and Catherine, the central characters in Hemingway's *A Farewell to Arms,* are in many

ways the doubles of Holden and Ameera. Hemingway
often acknowledged his literary indebtedness to Kipling,[21]
and while it is impossible to establish with any certainty
that the earlier story influenced the later, the parallels remain striking. Both couples find love outside the arbitrary
bounds which society has established for it, and both nur-
ture that love in a precarious world which threatens them
at every moment with separation and death. Both find an
almost idyllic happiness in the midst of a holocaust, both
are tantalized for a brief moment with the hope, which
they never quite permit themselves to believe in, of a normal existence, and in both cases the women die, leaving
the men to face life alone.

In theme as well as in plot structure, the stories are remarkably alike. Both Kipling and Hemingway, for example, draw the same conclusions in their stories about the
nature of life, conclusions which by now have become almost philosophical commonplaces of this century and
which are admirably epitomized in Albert Camus' vision
of an absurd universe, of which I will have more to say in
a later chapter. In this universe, in which there are only
two basic truths—man's desire for order and his knowledge
that he can never achieve it—the human being must learn
to live with the absurdity of this enormous contradiction
without, on the one hand, accepting the easy answers he
finds all about him, or, on the other, abandoning the search

---

21. He is quoted, for example, in *The New York Times* of 3 July
1961, p. 6, as having said that Kipling was very influential in the forming
of his style. He especially mentions the stories "At the End of the Passage" and "The Strange Ride of Morrowbie Jukes" in this connection. In
the following excerpt from "The Madness of Private Ortheris," Kipling's
style seems almost indistinguishable from Hemingway's. "Then we sat
down . . . by the side of the river, and took pot shots at the crocodiles in
the intervals of cutting up the food with our only pocket knife. Then we
drank up all the beer, and threw the bottles into the water and fired at
them. After that, we eased belts and stretched ourselves on the warm
sand and smoked. We were too lazy to continue shooting."

for meaning even when confronted with the certainty of failure in that search.

This position is precisely the one that is taken both in "Without Benefit of Clergy" and in *A Farewell to Arms*; taken with perhaps fewer overtones of self-pity in Kipling's story than in Hemingway's. For Ameera's insight at the end of her life is very much like Camus'. Having known a time when the reassurance of ritual had attracted her, she now sees the price that must be paid for such easy solace—the deadening of consciousness, the diminution of awareness and thus of joy. With considerable strength of will she rejects that comfort, and in the face of her sense of cosmic emptiness affirms the validity of human experience.

This act of Ameera's helps us to question the two generalizations about Kipling which are at least implicit in the usual readings of "Recessional." First it suggests that the writer was not, like the Kipling of popular legend, consistently contemptuous of, or even patronizing toward, Indian natives, but rather that he was, at his best, capable both of delineating and of judging Indians as individuals. Other stories confirm this open-mindedness. "Lisbeth," for instance, an early piece from *Plain Tales from the Hills* which depicts the cruelty of an Englishman toward an Indian girl, challenges the idea that Kipling "completely and conveniently forgot the hardships and humiliations that the Indians suffered at the hands of the British."[22] And *Kim*, by any literary standards a work of high quality, and Kipling's maturest study of India, successfully communicates—as much through its form as through the ideas it directly expresses—the author's sympathy for and understanding of the Eastern mind.

Kim begins and ends with the Lama; everything that happens in the story does so within a framework of the

---

22.   K. Bhaskara Rao, *Rudyard Kipling's India* (Norman, 1967), p. 10.

Lama's mystical quest for the River of the Arrow. At first, this quest does not seem to differ significantly from the quests of the other people encountered on the Grand Trunk Road. All men quest; it is in the nature of life to do so. The beggar looking for his evening meal, the Secret Service out to trap a spy as a part of the "Great Game," the Lama searching for his river are all one, or at least they seem to be. But by the end of the book it has begun to seem that all worldly quests are absurdly futile, since the triumphant conclusion of each search is only the beginning of the next. The Lama's quest alone seems real, for it is a quest for the end of all questing, and it is successful. In a trance, the soul of the holy man leaves its body and joins with the "oneness of creation." And looking back, the soul sees "the stupid body of Teshoo Lama lying down," sees the whole world of trivial acts it has left and knows them for what they are—games. They may be "Great Games"— Kipling certainly appreciates the skill of the players—but games they remain. The only reality for the Lama is the oneness which he has achieved, of which his love for Kim is a single manifestation.

Such a vision, though it may not have been one Kipling himself shared, is a grand one. It is the great vision of the orient, and that Kipling, with his western mind, should have been capable of so much understanding of it implies sympathy and not contempt for the mind of the East, a sympathy which may sometimes have faltered under the stress of the writer's own problems (as Edmund Wilson has noted) but which never entirely failed. For in a universe in which the lives of all men are equally ephemeral, at least a part of Kipling seems always to have believed that there are no permanently "lesser breeds," only those who temporarily lack understanding of "the Law."

Ameera's strong affirmation of self in "Without Benefit

of Clergy" also raises doubts about some traditional defi-
nitions of the word "Law"[23] as that word appears in Kipling's works. For Kipling seems as well aware in "Without
Benefit of Clergy" as in *Kim* that mere parliamentary legis-
lation is no more a meaningful equivalent of universal Law
than are rituals of magic and superstition. Holden and
Ameera make the same discovery. As they move through
the story, putting their faith first in one inadequate code
and then another, they come inevitably to the conclusion
that in a cosmos that offers no clear model for men to emu-
late, the only meaningful model must be man himself, and
faith in the validity of one's own experience the only meaningful law. For the player of games, for the builder of
bridges, for the questing Lama, the central requirement of
life is self-knowledge and fulfilment. Each must discover

---

23. The word "Law," appearing as it does frequently in Kipling's
work, has been looked on with nearly as much suspicion as the word
"breeds." Nor can the exact meaning of the term be established with any
finality (though many critics have tried), for Kipling spoke of the Law
in many different contexts and may even be said to have deliberately
avoided a precise definition of it. It is in part this ambiguity which has
disturbed those readers who see, in Kipling's repeated references to the
Law in his writings, another instance of the author's thoughtless celebration of the ritual of empire, one more sign of his complacency about the
British Raj and the white man's superior civilization. There are a number
of indications, however, that Kipling had something more universal than
the white man's dominion in mind when he used the word, many indications that the "Law," as it appears frequently in his work, is to be seen as
a kind of structure at the heart of things which must be discovered by
men rather than created by them, which has an existence apart from
man's awareness of it, which is, in short, descriptive rather than prescrip-
tive. The opening of one of the Mowgli stories in *The Jungle Books* makes
this point. "How Fear Came" begins:

The Law of the Jungle—which is by far the oldest law in the world—has
arranged for almost every kind of accident that may befall the Jungle-
People, till now its code is as perfect as time and custom can make it.

The "Law of the Jungle" is defined here quite clearly by the terms in
which it is discussed. It is spoken of as "the oldest law in the world," as
having been part, perhaps, of Creation itself. Moreover, it arranges for
accidents to befall the Jungle-People; it has a motive power, an existence
of its own and is not the invention of the animals. Kipling carefully dis-

that law within himself which represents the only universal
Law there is. Each confronts, in other words, what D. H.
Lawrence was to call "The burden of self-accomplishment!/The charge of fulfilment!"[24] And each, if he proves
equal to the task, measures up in his own way—the games-
man through his almost abstract skill at manipulating his
environment, the bridge-builder (as we shall see) through
his incarnation of self in an external object, and Teshoo
Lama through self-abnegation, abnegation at least of his
worldly self. The code which Ameera and Holden finally
devise is one which instructs them to "sit together and
laugh, calling each other openly by every pet name that
could move the wrath of the gods"; one which insists, that
is, that they be wholly themselves, that they freely follow
the Law of their own natures.

For Kipling, in other words, the "Law" of the universe
manifests itself most clearly and fully in the order and
necessity of each man's nature. In the last of the *Jungle
Book* stories, "The Spring Running," for instance, the pri-
mary Law of the Jungle is very specifically identified with
this "burden of self-accomplishment," with the obligation

---

tinguishes in this passage between "Law" and "code," the latter being the
rules or statutes which men, with the aid of time and custom, devise to
implement the Law. Codes, being man-made, can be wrong; the Law,
being inherent in the structure of the universe, cannot. This is why Kipling, with no intention at all of behaving in an autocratic or arbitrary way,
can say, as he frequently does in his writings, that the Law must always
be obeyed. For the obedience he requires is demanded not on some soul-
less, authoritarian principle, but rather because compliance with the Law,
as that word has been defined here, is synonymous with right knowledge
of the truth, with the necessary acceptance of "things as they are." Andre
Maurois has said of Kipling that his real significance resides in the fact
that "he has a permanent, natural contact with the oldest and deepest
layers of human consciousness," and it is only on such a level that the
author's use of the word "Law," in "Recessional" and elsewhere, is to be
fully understood.

24. D. H. Lawrence, "Humiliation," *Complete Poems*, ed. Pinto &
Roberts, Vol. I (New York, 1964), p. 215.

of every organism to discover and fulfill itself. Mowgli has spent his whole life among animals, learning their ways. But as he approaches manhood he begins to find that he is not himself like the animals. His eyes have shown this from the beginning, but in this last tale the point is made most explicitly.

... the look in [Mowgli's] eyes was always gentle. Even when he fought, his eyes never blazed as Bagheera's did. They only grew more and more interested and excited. . . .

Mowgli is not an animal; he is himself, a man, and because of this he must leave the jungle and return to men. The boy has passed through a preliminary training which is, in many respects, like the preliminary training appropriate for animals. But finally the moment comes for him to move beyond his brothers, and it is precisely his discovery of this truth about himself and, even more important, his obedience to that truth, which sets him apart, as it sets Holden and Ameera—and the Lama, the bridge-builder and even the players of the Great Game—apart from the boastful, false-hearted *Bandar-log* of the world, the "lesser breeds without the Law."

But the Law, in the sense in which I have been using the word here, is as applicable to works of art as it is to men, is as much an aesthetic Law as it is a social and political one, as much the Law of art as the Law of nature. Indeed, the terms in which I have been discussing Ameera's and Mowgli's self-discoveries are the same terms in which earlier I talked about "Recessional." That poem, I said, is an aesthetic failure because it never quite finds its own voice, never achieves wholeness; because, ironically, it is itself "without the Law." "Without Benefit of Clergy," on the other hand, succeeds as a work of art precisely because of its coherence of structure and metaphor. The proof of its success is that the reader is never tempted, as he is in "Recessional," to go outside the work to find terms for understanding it. No pre-existent attitude toward imperialism, for example, is required here as it is in the poem. Indeed, in the context of "Without Benefit of Clergy" such an attitude would be irrelevant. Outside the context of the story, it might be possible to make the point that since the British—including Holden—had no business being in India in the first place, Ameera's suffering is all unnecessary, quite gratuitous. But it is difficult to imagine even the most dedicated anti-imperialist making such a remark about this work. The story itself does not raise the issue, and it is one sign of a successful story that issues which do not exist in the world created by the story do not—for the time we are reading the work and hearing its voice—exist at all.

We know that Kipling was himself not always true to the Law of his own nature, as that Law is expressed in his most serious poems and stories, and that it was with these aesthetic failures that he invited the familiar political and sociological attacks on his work. Yet to some extent the patronizing of other races in the poorer works, the snobbery there, is no more than a kind of (grossly, of course) exaggerated impatience with those who have not fully achieved themselves, a kind of impatience which could be directed with equal fervor, as we have seen, against the foolish Member from Lower Tooting or the poorer-spirited wives of the English colony. Furthermore, from his best stories—to which we naturally pay most attention—a Kipling emerges whose vision of life is deeper, more complicated and much more worth attending to than that of the comic villain of the Beerbohm caricatures. When he followed that deeper vision, when he found his own voice, as he did in "Without Benefit of Clergy," Kipling never wrote of lesser *races*, and if he spoke of lesser *breeds*, he clearly had in mind the sort of breeding which, in his view, men and women—as well as works of art—can achieve only by implementing the Law they discover in and for themselves.

CHAPTER THREE ✵

The Art of the Simple

i

My discussion of the structure of "Without Benefit of Clergy" and of the aesthetic implications of its theme perhaps assumes the existence of a greater degree of sophistication in Kipling's art than many readers are accustomed to finding there. To be sure, W. H. Auden made the famous statement that "Time that. . ./Pardoned Kipling and his views,/And will pardon Paul Claudel,/Pardons [them] for writing well. . ." but a number of readers today would disagree, not so much with the idea that Kipling might conceivably be pardoned for his views as with the idea that Kipling did, in fact, write well. Certainly, the author of "Mandalay" and "Gunga Din" still seems to many today to be no more than an extraordinarily skillful journalist, a best-selling, slightly vulgar entertainer, rather than a serious artist. And his continuing success with popular book clubs, which regularly offer leather-bound, gold-tooled sets of the works of Kipling as inducements to membership, simply reinforces his reputation as one who writes well only in a narrow commercial sense and not at all in Auden's more rarefied sense. Thus, before I go on with critical readings which presuppose a high order of artistic maturity in Kipling's stories, it might be useful to pause and examine the familiar assumption that Kipling did not possess such maturity.

Even in the early eighteen-nineties, when the writer was just beginning to make his literary reputation, much criticism of his works centered around what were then regarded as inadequacies in his style. By some readers the young author was taken to task for what was considered the insufferably knowing tone of some of his stories, for his complacent, almost vulgar clubbiness, for his transparent attempts to seem a blasé insider, privy to every sort of official secret. To others, his pieces, especially those in *Plain Tales from the Hills*, seemed too journalistic, too breezy in presentation, too slap-dash and chatty. "The style," C. E. Carrington writes, "is that of the gossip-column."[1] The charge could safely be made, since much of Kipling's work, up to the time of his first appearance in London, had been done in his capacity as newspaper reporter and editor and since most of the pieces in *Plain Tales* had originally been written to order as filler for *The Civil and Military Gazette*.

Still, the criticism is a reasonable one, for Kipling often appeared to be taking the easy way out in his narratives, intruding himself baldly into his tales in order to save time, addressing his readers directly, explaining instead of dramatizing. Indeed, this habit of including himself in the cast of characters of his own stories earned him some of his harshest rebukes. The nine-days wonder of the literary world seemed to many critics to be, in the words of Francis Adams, "full of sickening egotism and vanity," no more, in short, than "a little-brained second-rate journalist,"[2] a phrase which strikingly anticipates the judgment of a large percentage—perhaps even a majority—of sophisticated readers today. It may be worth while, however, consider-

---

1. C. E. Carrington, *The Life of Rudyard Kipling* (New York, 1955), p. 69.
2. Quoted by Hilton Brown in *Rudyard Kipling* (New York, 1945), p. 30.

52   *The Good Kipling*

ing with care one or two of Kipling's more apparently trivial and "second-rate" journalistic endeavors, for while the
negative view of much of this work predominates among
intellectuals, as sensitive a reader as James Joyce is known
to have felt that the "little-brained" and gossipy-seeming
Plain Tales from the Hills showed "more promise than any
other contemporary writer's youthful work."[3]

Any one of the pieces from *Plain Tales*, chosen at random, would serve our purpose, but ideally, we ought to
consider a tale which Adams himself might have selected
as a good example of the sort of simple-minded journalism
which Kipling supposedly produced during his apprentice
years. "The Arrest of Lt. Golightly" is such a story. It is
hardly a profound tale and is certainly not the most memorable of the forty vignettes in the collection. It has never
had any critical consideration, as some of the other stories
in the book have, nor is there anything particularly surprising about this neglect. The episode in which Lieutenant
Golightly figures seems little more than a "slight anecdote,"[4] as Professor Carrington has called it, a farcical in-
terlude, a joke.

The plot of the little tale is not difficult to summarize.
Lieutenant Golightly, a young British officer and dandy
serving in India, sets out on horseback from Dalhousie, a
hill station where he has been on leave, to return to his
duty assignment in the plain. Along the way he runs into
a torrential rain which ruins his clothes and so alters his
appearance that he is mistaken for a runaway enlisted man
and suffers extravagantly before the matter is finally
straightened out. There is nothing more to the story than
that. It is no wonder that the critics have never had any-

3. Richard Ellmann, *James Joyce* (New York, 1959), p. 673 (note).
4. Carrington, p. 82.

thing to say about it. There doesn't seem to be anything to say.

Yet for all its slightness, "The Arrest of Lieutenant Golightly" is a wonderfully artful piece of work. Analysis of it shows that Kipling had this early found not only the subject matter of his later fiction,[5] but also the major themes; and that even at the beginning of his career he was already a quite conscious artist, skillful at embodying an idea in action without sacrificing any of that action's ability to entertain. For example, what is important about Lieutenant Golightly is that he is a young man whose special nature it is to see and deal with the world superficially. His ticket name suggests as much, and we are not surprised to learn that the young officer is proud of his ability to get through life in "light marching-order." His preoccupation with clothes is the most immediate indication of his character. Traditionally in literature, an obsession with personal appearance and especially with clothing is the mark of a superficial man, usually of a man who must be taught a lesson. Kipling is obviously writing in this tradition, and he reinforces our impression of Golightly by introducing him at once as a man who is proud—that word appears often in the story—of "looking like 'an officer and a gentleman.'" Of *looking* like an officer and a gentleman. Appearances would seem to be quite enough for Golightly, at least at first. By the end of the story we will find

---

5. In the process of telling this anecdote, Kipling manages to include, if only by oblique reference, nearly every aspect of life in India which he was later to expand into full-length stories. The tale is first of all about a young British officer in India, a favorite subject. In passing, however, it also touches on leave at hill stations, life on the road, native officials, unreliable native servants, Indian railroads and railroad stations, the British enlisted man, the congenial, tradition-ridden, gossipy officers' mess, and even that character who appears mistily in the background of so much Kipling fiction, Kipling himself. On this last point, we shall have more to say later.

him, foolish and unaware as ever, taking exactly the opposite stand without at all knowing what he is doing.

This superficiality of Golightly's, symbolized by his passion for clothes, is further dramatized by the trip from Dalhousie to the railway station at Pathankote. Golightly's notions about how the universe works seem to be as light-headed as his ideas about clothes making the man. The lieutenant prides himself on his "faculty of organization," but the plans he makes require for their success a sweetly reasonable and orderly world, more than anxious to be subdued. And such a world, Kipling would have us understand, does not exist; anyone, he says repeatedly in his best stories, who fails to see that the universe is a chaotic, irrational place, hostile to man, and who fails to come to terms with that universe, is certain to suffer.[6] And no one more certain than Lieutenant Golightly, whose whole style of life, like the helmet that he wears, is made for sunny days and collapses grotesquely in the rain.

Golightly, ready to start on his trip, makes plans for the superficial world of his own invention, plans designed to save him trouble and to help him travel in light marching-order. But no sooner has he set out on his journey than the-world-as-it-really-is begins to encroach on these plans. Almost at once, and quite unreasonably, clouds appears and begin to produce a "good, tepid, monsoonish downpour." Golightly has not, of course, included an umbrella in his plans, but he consoles himself with the thought of the fresh clothes and the supply of money he has cleverly sent on

---

6. In "Kipling—The Theme of Vanity," *English Studies Today*, 3rd series (Edinburgh, 1964), J. M. S. Tompkins says about *The Light that Failed*: "The punishment that Dick accepts is a nemesis in the nature of things; the powers which Kipling never defines, but always acknowledges . . ." p. 175. The appropriateness of this passage to our discussion here is plain. Miss Tompkins' insight is also central, however, to our entire investigation of Kipling's art.

ahead with his servant. Unfortunately, the delightful perversity of that servant is also no part of Golightly's plan. "He did not know . . . that his *khitmatgar* would stop by the roadside to get drunk, and would come on the next day saying that he had sprained his ankle." Thus the universe is quick to punish Golightly for his presumption, and to punish him in a most appropriate way. Item by item it destroys the clothes of which he is so inordinately and foolishly fond and in the act of destroying them reveals their shoddiness.

The thematic use which Kipling makes of this episode may help to explain why he lavished such care on his description of Golightly's undoing, why every detail of the disintegration is so lovingly presented. The plot of the story requires a complete alteration in Golightly's appearance, and so Kipling must do his best to make the later confusion of identities plausible by describing elaborately the effects of the monsoon on the lieutenant's clothes. But more important, it is the gross inadequacy of Golightly's style of life, and certainly not any sadistic penchant on Kipling's part for making people uncomfortable, which produces the young officer's very special and picturesque disaster. The author obviously relishes the scene, but the description throughout is good-natured and the final phrase quite charming. "The effect," Kipling writes of the mingling of purple and green dyes on the lieutenant's face and neck, "was amazing."

The transformation of the proud, handsome young officer of Dalhousie into the filthy, nearly naked apparition who struggles on foot into Pathankote is only the first of many ironic reversals which Kipling presents in the course of his story. Golightly has not been in town long, for example, when he is mistaken for a runaway army private, is arrested in the act of arranging for a railway ticket by the Station-Master and four constables, and begins to receive some unpleasant instruction in the old adage about what happens to men who live by the sword. For the Station-Master and the constables are, like the young officer, also men who believe in the importance of appearances, and the one thing they are absolutely certain of is "that no lieutenant could look such a ruffian as did Golightly." Golightly begins to shout at his captors but only succeeds in confirming their suspicions. " 'Without doubt this is the soldier-Englishman we require,' " says the Station-Master. " 'Listen to the abuse!' "

The lieutenant is ignominiously bundled off and placed in the custody of a military search party whose members have been out looking for one Private John Binkel, deserter, and who now imagine that they have found him. And here the story takes an even more amusing turn. For as long as Golightly tries to maintain the artificial dignity of the officer he really is, the corporal and the two privates are disgusted. "This is a very absurd mistake, my men," Golightly begins priggishly, but his explanation is quickly interrupted. "*You* a orficer," says the corporal. "It's the like o' *you* as brings disgrace on the likes of *us*. Bloomin' fine orficer you are!" Which, in its convoluted way, is a not wholly unreasonable thing to say about the young lieutenant.

The moment, however, that Golightly, in his frustration, begins to shout and swear "like a trooper," he wins his captors over completely, all the while, of course, convincing them even further that he is the runaway private they have been looking for.

"I've heard a few beggars in the clink blind, stiff and crack on a bit; but I've never 'eard anyone to touch this 'ere orficer,' " [says one of the men.] They were not angry with him. They rather admired him. They had some beer at the refreshment room, and offered Golightly some too, because he had 'swore wonderful.'

The irony of all this, clearly, is that at last, and quite by chance, the reader has gotten down to something in Golightly that is real, that isn't a matter of illusion or appearance. For at bottom, it seems, Golightly is neither an officer nor a gentlemen, despite his elaborate efforts to look the part. What he really is becomes plain in this small crisis, and instantly the reality is recognized and the young lieutenant is gathered into the honest fellowship of the privates and the corporal. It is at this point that the mistaken identity is most outrageous, but, paradoxically, it is also at this point that Golightly is most truly and most appealingly himself.

Not that he knows it. Golightly is extraordinarily ignorant of the reasons for his own behavior. We have seen that when he acts, it is never on any sort of intelligent principle but only out of a concern for personal convenience. Thus his travel plans have nothing whatever to do with the realities of life on the road, but are designed solely to permit him to hurry along beautifully dressed and in unburdened comfort. Nor is his dandyism based on any strong conviction about the importance of appearances in life. Even worldliness can be elevated to the level of principle, but Golightly is a dandy only because dressing well is the most pleasant and least uncomfortable way he has found of demonstrating that he is an officer and a gentleman. This fact is plain from the way he handles himself in his crisis. Anyone powerfully committed to dandyism would, in Golightly's disreputable condition, have crept into town in an agony of self-consciousness, imagining, no doubt, that natives of the lowest caste were cutting him dead in the street.

Not so Golightly. No sooner does he arrive in Pathankote

than he begins to go about his business as if nothing had happened to him. He looks for his servant, he orders a drink, he negotiates with the Station-Master for a ticket to Khasa, and a first-class ticket at that. This dandy, for whom, only a few hours before, appearances had been everything, now behaves as if he were wholly unaware of his own villainous appearance and, what's more, as if everyone else were unaware of it too. This is the cream of Kipling's jest. Golightly, under the pressure of circumstances, has shifted his ground. He has conveniently forgotten about the importance of *looking* like an officer and a gentleman and now takes the position that there is such a thing as a pure essence of gentlemanliness, which he clearly possesses and which ought to be asserting itself in spite of his unpromising appearance. So firmly does he maintain this position that in the end he passes the greater part of the summer "trying to get the corporal and the two soldiers tried by court-martial for arresting an 'officer and a gentleman.'"

Superbly unconscious throughout his adventure, Golightly is funny because he so determinedly fails to learn the truth either about himself or about the way the world works. The truth about Golightly we have already seen. The truth about the world is, even in this slight anecdote, extremely complex, but Kipling gives us a clue to his vision of it in the story itself. When Golightly first arrives in Pathankote, he buys a drink and pays eight annas for it. "This revealed to him that he had only six annas more in his pocket—*or in the world as he stood at that hour*" (italics mine). The phrase is a significant one. "The Arrest of Lieutenant Golightly" is crowded with accidents and mistakes, with illustrations, as it were, of the randomness and irrationality of the universe, and in such a universe it is axiomatic that any sort of elaborate planning will be useless. True, Golightly's plans are foolish because they are irresponsible, but we might easily imagine, under the same circumstances, a man on horseback loaded down with monsoon equipment and changes of clothing looking quite as foolish. When we see people carrying umbrellas on sunny days, our first thought is not that they are wise and provident planners but rather that they look ridiculous. Yet their only mistake has been to guess wrong about the weather, and they might just as easily have guessed right.

Kipling is obviously not opposed to planning in itself, though in such stories as "A Germ Destroyer" he humorously warns against a mere proliferation of policy which may make a man inflexible in the face of new challenges. His real point, however, is that the universe, in its fortuitousness, is always able to come up with some unexpected challenge for which no amount of planning could have prepared, and that in such an hour, all a man has in the world is what, figuratively speaking, he has in his pockets. And what he ought to have in his pockets for such a time is precisely what Lieutenant Golightly does not have and for the lack of which he is "arrested" in mid-career, a consciousness of the truth about himself—the only universally useful tool in an uncertain world.[7]

A shock is in store for readers who turn from this explication of "The Arrest of Lieutenant Golightly" to the story itself. The tale or anecdote is so light-weight that the solemnity of the analysis seems out of all proportion to the slenderness of the subject. Yet there need be no correlation between a narrative's solemnity (or lack of it) and its structural complexity, and indeed, it is precisely because

7. One critic makes a convincing case for the idea that this is one of the central themes of the whole of *Plain Tales from the Hills*. See Louis Cornell, *Kipling in India* (New York, 1966), p. 135. "No one in India," he writes, "is entirely free from the delusions caused by false appearances; on every hand pitfalls await the foolish or the over-confident."

"The Arrest of Lieutenant Golightly" is so innocent of conscious "serious" intentions that it was picked for consideration here. For what its constructional sophistication reveals is that Kipling, young as he was when he wrote his tale, and pressured as he was by a newspaper deadline, was nevertheless able to handle even such admittedly slight material as this like an artist, to give even these stock elements of farce a single center and a serious theme. Thus, though some of his work may have been journalistic in style and subject, the author must not, in the light of a story such as this, be dismissed as a mere journalist.

ii

The charge of journalistic simple-mindedness is, however, only a part of Francis Adams' attack on the writer. There remains, for example, the matter of what Adams has called Kipling's "sickening vanity," a quality which might well make him, if not a second-rate journalist, then a second-rate artist. In order to evaluate this judgment it would be useful to look at still another work from *Plain Tales from the Hills*, this time one entirely dependent, for the communication of its theme, upon just those elements of blasé knowingness, of adolescent smugness which have seemed repellent to critics and readers for the last three-quarters of a century.

In none of the forty stories in *Plain Tales from the Hills* does the intrusion of the author seem more gratuitous nor the character which goes under the author's name more callow than in "In the House of Suddhoo." The unpleasantness begins in the first paragraph. After introducing the principal participants in his little drama, Kipling adds, as a grotesquely coy afterthought, "Then there is Me, of course; but I am only the chorus that comes in at the end to explain things. So I do not count." Surely, it would be difficult to imagine more heavy-handed irony than this. Nor, though it appears in the initial paragraph, is this passage the first example in the story of that "egotism and vanity" which Adams decries. Even earlier in the tale, Kipling finds an opportunity to brag about his connections. "Suddhoo is a great friend of mine," he explains off-handedly, "because his cousin had a son who secured, thanks to my recommendation, the post of head-messenger to a big firm in the station."

This last is a key to all of Kipling's remarks in the story, for throughout the narrative the author seems much more concerned with making an impression than with recounting the incidents of his tale. At any rate, he does not hesitate to interrupt the drama with knowing asides whenever an opportunity arises for a little self-aggrandizement. Talking with Suddhoo, for example, at an agonizing moment in the old man's life, Kipling cannot resist making a worldly-wise comment about the ways of the British Government in India, a comment which he must know Suddhoo will not understand but which obviously strikes him as too clever to omit.

I said that so far from magic being discouraged by the Government, it was highly commended. The greatest Officials of the state practised it themselves. (If the Financial Statement isn't magic, I don't know what it is.)

Just as embarrassing as this feeble attempt at insider's wit is the little literary lesson which the author intrudes into the very middle of his most exciting scene. Nowhere does Kipling sound more like a self-important schoolboy than when he is recommending to his readers that they look into "Poe's account of the voice that came from the mesmerized dying man." Even the failure to identify the story further is provoking.[8]

---

8.   The allusion is to "The Facts in the Case of M. Valdemar." In her book, *Kipling's Reading* (Philadelphia, 1939), Ann M. Weygandt points

Obviously, the Kipling who marches stiffly, complacently, and ludicrously through the story is a foolish young man, playing at being a *sahib*. His informal chattiness with his readers is offensive; we do not want to be included "in." His designation of Janoo and Azizun as "Ladies of the City" who ply "an ancient and more or less honorable profession" is unpleasantly arch. His faith in the efficacy of British Law is absurd. And his little joke about Suddhoo failing to send proper transportation for a future Lieutenant-Governor falls flat because we can easily imagine the author being genuinely offended at the omission. In short, if ever a case could be made for the standard criticism of Kipling's early work, "In The House of Suddhoo" seems to make that case. Here are all the flaws at their worst: the blatant intrusion of the author, the breezy journalistic style, the intellectual and social pretension.

Having said all this about the story, however, we must add that "In the House of Suddhoo" remains a fine and effective piece of work. Some critics[9] have even thought it one of Kipling's finest tales, and in fact it is difficult to imagine anyone reading it without being caught up in the details of its action, without being impressed by the seriousness of its theme. The wonder is that this brief narrative should seem so successful with all the flaws we have noted, that the obtuse and insensitive Kipling who appears as the narrator of the story should also have been capable of the precise and brilliant description of the seal-cutter's magic. Indeed, the contradictions are so gross that they

out, with reference to Kipling's remark about the "voice that came from the mesmerized dying man," that "the man was already dead when his voice was at its ghastliest." (p. 147) This is, of course, an extremely minor point, interesting only for the way in which it contributes to the impression of the narrator's superficiality. In all likelihood, however, the error was an unconscious one on Kipling's part.

9. Stephen Vincent Benet, for one, in "Rudyard Kipling, Teller of Magic Tales," *New York Herald Tribune Books*, XII (12 Jan. 1936), 1-2.

force us to re-examine our first impressions. For either "In the House of Suddhoo" is not nearly so good as it seems, or the ridiculous figure which the young Kipling cuts in the story, so far from detracting from the tale, actually contributes to its success.

The question we must face in seeking a solution to this problem is, of course, one that is raised by every story in which the author is himself a participant in the action: to what extent are the author and the narrator identical? One position in this matter is implicit in the traditional view of Kipling as a brash egotist. "The 'I' of these stories," says a critic of this persuasion, is "Kipling himself, Kipling the journalist, not a mere idealized projection of his own personality."[10] It is just this assertion, however—that the young man who tells the story is in fact the author's mouthpiece and that readers must take this young man quite seriously when he speaks or acts—which leaves us with an irreconcilable contradiction between the callowness of the author and the effectiveness of the tale.

Nothing obliges us, though, to be so dogmatic about identifying the narrator with the author in Kipling's early works, especially "In The House of Suddhoo." It may very well be, for example, that the young man who speaks to us from the pages of that story is quite distinct from the young man who wrote those pages; it may be that the consciousness of the narrator, so far from occupying the moral center of the tale, is itself part of the larger and more discriminating consciousness of the author, a consciousness eminently capable of passing judgment on its fictional alter ego. In this view the "I" of the story is not Kipling himself, "Kipling the journalist," but one of the story's characters, a figure whose ideas do not necessarily represent those of

10.   Walter M. Hart, *Kipling the Story-Writer* (Berkeley, 1918), p. 34.

the author and whose function in the narrative is to help
dramatize the theme of the work and not simply to propa-
gandize it.[11] At the very least such a view seems worth considering, if only because the moment we do so, the problem
raised by the disparity between the story's quality and
Kipling's apparent insensitivity vanishes.

It is not, we now see, Kipling the author but rather Kipling the narrator who is ridiculously callow; not the real
Kipling but Kipling the fictional character who struts self-
importantly through the tale, patronizing all the people he
meets. The distinction is a significant one, for if we accept
it, what had once seemed a flaw in the narrative, a destructive intrusion of the author into his work, begins to
emerge for what it really is—a vehicle for the communication of the story's theme. Indeed, the whole force of the
irony of this tale depends upon our being able to differenti-
ate between the narrator of the story, who, until the last
moment, understands nothing of what is going on, and the
story's author, who understands, and who helps us to understand, everything.

Kipling develops the theme of his story with a sure touch
out of the conflict between his complacent young narrator
and the teeming land of India, a land which, in a minor and
peripheral way, the young man helps to govern. In such a
brief story as this there is hardly room for an entire sub-
continent; instead, Kipling has arranged for his description of a single house to convey the impression of a whole
world. The mention of Poe later in the story may remind
us that the word "house" has metaphoric overtones suggestive of dynasties or of whole countries, but the picture
of the House of Suddhoo which the author presents makes
the same point without literary allusions. Indeed, the two-

11.   See Louis Cornell's discussion of this same point in his *Kipling in
India*, p. 130 ff.

storied, flat-roofed, white-washed building seems to offer, just among its occupants, a cross-section of everyday Indian life. "Bhagwan Dass the grocer," Kipling writes, "and a man who says he gets his living by seal-cutting live in the lower story with a troop of wives, servants, friends and retainers." The upper rooms are occupied by Janoo and Azizun, two Kashmiri "Ladies of the City," and Suddhoo, the toothless, feeble-minded owner of the establishment "sleeps on the roof generally, except when he sleeps in the street." Thus the House of Suddhoo, to which the young narrator undertakes, with great if misguided self-confidence, to bring the benefits of Western Law and decorum, seems to represent, in miniature, the swarming world of India to which other Englishmen have come with similar laudable designs.

The description we get of the House of Suddhoo comes, of course, from the narrator. This is plain in the second sentence of the story when the young man, requiring a phrase to describe the five red hand-prints which decorate an outer wall of the house, speaks of them as being arranged like "the five of diamonds." The image, drawn as it is from the card-room of the Club, is a revealing one. It establishes the fact, at the very beginning of the tale, that the narrator's deepest instinct is to convert his experiences with the strange people of this exotic land into familiar terms, into comforting western terms with which he can feel at home and which he is confident he can handle. And it is this instinct, and the inappropriateness of the responses which it inspires, that provides the substance of the story.

The narrator clearly has no sense of this inappropriateness when the story opens, and here we have one instance of how his callowness contributes to the ironic telling of the tale. For approached by Suddhoo in the matter of the seal-cutter's magic, he first indulges in his little insider's joke and then, with his usual ebullient self-confidence, re-assures the old man that all will be well. Strangely enough, it does not seem to bother the narrator in the least that he is ignorant of the law about which Suddhoo has particularly come to consult him. Indeed, so much a representative of British rule does he feel himself, and so certain is he of the efficacy of that rule, that he magisterially gives his own permission for the magic to proceed—"I had not the least objection to giving it my countenance and sanction"—and, announcing that he himself understands a little magic "in the Western line," promises rather pompously to go with Suddhoo to his house to see that everything is done "decently and in order."

In this off-handed way, then, and with perfect confidence in the invincibility of his reason and in the power of the British Raj, the young narrator enters into the House of Suddhoo to judge the evil-doers he may find there and to protect the innocent from harm. Nor does he change his plans significantly once he has come face to face with the seal-cutter's magic. He is no doubt affected by the sheer flamboyance of the sights he sees, but his mind is always working to expose the fraud he is certain is being perpetrated, and he always discovers the flaw in the performance: the twitching of a muscle that has nothing to do with respiration, or the fire-breathing trick that he himself knows how to do. Thus, in the end, the theatrical display leaves him unmoved and his faith in the Englishman's ability to control situations of this sort unshaken. With a half-pitying, half-contemptuous glance at Suddhoo, crumpled on the floor in a paroxysm of terror, the young narrator turns to the clear-thinking Janoo "to discuss the probabilities of the whole thing being a *bunao*, or 'make-up.'" And finally, having convinced himself that there is no mystery in the House of Suddhoo that cannot be cleared up with a little judicious exercise of authority—an attitude not shared, naturally, by the writer of the story—he utters the words which he has no doubt been holding in reserve all evening—" 'Of course I can speak to the seal-cutter, and he shall refund' "—and in that moment his whole orderly world begins to collapse around him.

For hardly are his confident words out of his mouth when the significance of Janoo's earlier statement strikes him. " 'This seal-cutter man is a liar and a devil,' " the woman had warned.

"I dare not tell, do anything, or get anything done, because I am in debt to Bhagwan Dass the *bunnia* for two gold rings and a heavy anklet. I must get my food from his shop. The seal-cutter is the friend of Bhagwan Dass, and he would poison my food."

It is for this reason, Janoo points out, for the sake of her own life, that nothing must be said or done about the seal-cutter's ingenious swindling of Suddhoo. But even as she speaks these words, the truth is dawning on the narrator of the trap into which he has fallen. For if a report from him automatically dooms Janoo to death at the hands of the seal-cutter, his silence, he now realizes, is equally deadly, for it guarantees the seal-cutter's death at the hands of the desperate Janoo. In short, what the young Englishman now sees is that no action of his can possibly be of any use, and that the world, which only a moment before had seemed to him so absolutely subject to his personal decisions, has gone veering off out of control, carrying its would-be Lieutenant-Governor with it.[12]

12.   Cornell suggests that the theme of this story is "the inability of the British to cope with their Indian subjects." (p. 113.) See also such tales as "Naboth," "The Story of Muhammad Din," and "The Strange Ride of Morrowbie Jukes" for the development of a similar theme.

It is, of course, humiliating enough for a man who has always thought of himself as a master-shaper of events to recognize that all along he has been only the insignificant instrument of fate. What is still more painful, however, is for him to realize that he has been everybody else's instrument as well. Yet this is precisely the humbling experience which has been reserved for the narrator; indeed, the story —always under the full control of the author—makes the point very clearly that neither the young man nor the way of life which he represents, and of which he is so proud, has ever been anything more than a convenient tool for the people who live in the House of Suddhoo. The telegraph, for example, that much-vaunted symbol of British ingenuity and supremacy, has become, in the seal-cutter's hands, just another trick in a profession that is nearly as ancient as Janoo's, while the narrator himself, flattered far past his ability to resist by the ostensibly feeble-minded Suddhoo, has allowed himself to be seduced into lending respectability to a, for him, altogether questionable business and into breaking one of his own laws as well. No wonder that the pictures of the Queen and the Prince of Wales, peering down from the walls of Janoo's room, seem "to heighten the grotesqueness" of the scene. For like the young Englishman present and, by extension, like all the Englishmen in India, they are able to watch the strange performance that is taking place but—for all their majesty —can do nothing to change a single moment of it.

The scene which the royal portraits witness is one of Kipling's most brilliantly drawn; the descriptions of the seal-cutter's gyrations and of his special effects are grim enough for the most chilling of supernatural tales. It is important to notice, therefore, that "In the House of Suddhoo" is *not* a story of the supernatural. True, Kipling might seem to have had every reason for introducing supernatural elements into his narrative. His hero is an arrogant young man, smugly certain that he knows all the answers and obviously ripe for enlightenment. What better way to call into question all of his complacent and orderly notions about the world and to establish the disturbingly different rhythm of Indian life than by arranging for him to experience a moment of pure terror in a native setting, a moment which he cannot rationally explain away?

The trouble with such a scheme, apart from its obviousness, is that it would force the author to say just the opposite of what he wanted to say, would oblige him to portray India as a world full of ghosts confounding the paltry rationality of the English. In fact, of course, the India of "In the House of Suddhoo" is overrun not by ghosts but by charlatans preying on men who believe in ghosts, and rationality, so far from being a drawback for the English in such a setting, is their most powerful weapon. (It is no accident, for example, that the young narrator of the story is at his best when he is looking coldly past the cheap theatricality of the seal-cutter's tricks to their simple explanations.)

Kipling's point, however, is that the true challenge of India lies not in such clumsy and readily exposed fakery as this but in the real world of grocers and prostitutes and feeble old men. It is in this world, the author wants us to understand, and not in the world of the supernatural that real terror and mystery are to be found, and it is for this world that the narrator's smug self-confidence, his patronizing air, his jokes and his literary allusions, are most inappropriate. Laws and mechanical contrivances he is brilliantly able to handle, but the deadly intimacies of the House of Suddhoo amaze him, appall him and finally trap him beyond any power of his to escape. His mere presence in the house compromises him. The very touch of life taints him. Turning from the fake exoticism of the seal-cutter's magic, he is plunged suddenly into the real exoticism of India, a thoroughly unromantic exoticism, product of crowded houses, cheap life, and hopelessly complex relationships, and he comes to understand for the first time the nature of the world in which he has lived for so long, so complacently.

Needless to say, there is no touch of that complacency in the last paragraph of the story. There, as the narrator tries to evaluate his experiences in the House of Suddhoo, his tone is almost solemn, as if he himself cannot yet believe what has happened to him, cannot yet appreciate the extent of the trap into which he has fallen. On the one hand, he points out, he stands convicted by his own law of abetting a fraud. On the other, he is trapped by the torturedly intricate human relationships with which, unthinkingly, he has become involved. The utter finality of that involvement is best summed up in the last sentence of the story. "And thus," the young Englishman writes, concluding the adventure he had entered upon so lightly, "I shall be privy to a murder in the House of Suddhoo."

iii

If, through these brief considerations of two early stories, I have been able to cast some doubt on the theory that Kipling was too simple and superficial a person to be a real artist, I can perhaps best conclude the discussion by examining—also briefly—a companion notion, the idea that the writer's subject matter was frequently too elementary to sustain serious works of art. The best-known purveyor of this idea was Henry James.

In his earliest time [James wrote in 1897 to Grace Norton] I thought [Kipling] perhaps contained the seeds of an English Balzac; but I have given that up in proportion as he has come

down steadily from the simple in subject to the more simple—
from the Anglo-Indians to the natives, from the natives to the
Tommies, from the Tommies to the quadrupeds, from the
quadrupeds to the fish, and from the fish to the engines and
screws.

James' position in this often-quoted criticism of Kipling is
not particularly strong. Not only is it absurd to imagine
that "natives" or "Tommies" are somehow inherently "simpler" subjects than Anglo-Indians, but it is also foolish to
suppose that the animal story—the beast epic or fable,
which has its own long and honorable history—cannot be
assimilated into the labyrinthine house of modern fiction.
No one can read *The Jungle Books*, for example, without
becoming aware of the almost Jamesian subtlety of some
of the relationships which Kipling describes, and without
becoming aware, too, that while the animals in the work
are depicted largely as animals and not as disguised men,
the story of the growth and development of Mowgli makes
of *The Jungle Books* a first rate example of a kind of book
that was quite popular in the late nineteenth and early
twentieth centuries—the *bildungsroman*.

Ordinarily, the *bildungsroman* deals with the inner
growth of a young person—with his efforts to come to terms
with the world as he finds it and to discover his own real
nature—in the context of conventional human society; thus
James is perhaps to be forgiven for not seeing in *The Jungle
Books* a resolution of the *bildungsroman* into its central
and crucial elements. Yet Kipling actually achieved such
a resolution, just as Defoe, in *Robinson Crusoe*, accom-
plished in his day a reduction to its central elements of
the then popular novel of a young person confronting the
world with no more than his natural endowments and successfully subduing it. Indeed, *The Jungle Books* function
as a *bildungsroman* in two different ways. First, they deal

F

more or less conventionally with the childhood and adolescence of Mowgli, with his growth from semi-animal jungle boyhood to civilized manhood. More than this, however, *The Jungle Books*—which have sometimes seemed to critics to be, in part, a pastiche of unrelated tales—reinforce the central *bildungsroman* elements in the Mowgli story with a series of independent narratives, each of which focuses rather specifically on one of these elements.

Every *bildungsroman* concerns itself, either directly or by implication, with two crucial moments in the inner life of its protagonist: first, the young hero's breaking away from the deadly "safety" of his father's house to face the challenging hostility of the world, and second, the young hero's rediscovery of his father in himself. The recognition that he is both uniquely himself and yet part of all that has gone before is the protagonist's great achievement in the *bildungsroman* (in any given novel that recognition may or may not occur, may or may not be considered a good thing), and it is certainly Mowgli's achievement in *The Jungle Books*. In addition to the Mowgli stories, though—and as if to illuminate them—Kipling has been at some pains in the book to embody the two crucial acts of the *bildungsroman* in the subsidiary tales.

"How Fear Came," for instance, is a retelling of the expulsion from Eden story, itself a *bildungsroman* archetype with its picture of Adam and Eve defying God and going out to make their own way in the world. Once, according to the tale Kipling tells, the jungle had been a peaceful place. Animals did not eat each other, and the lions (and tigers) quite literally lay down with the lambs. But then the lazy animals fell to quarreling over their food, though there was plenty for all, and in one of the many disputes that arose, the First of the Tigers accidentally killed a buck and brought death into being. All the elements of the Gar-

den of Eden myth are here: the perfect peace and innocence of the world at its birth, the act of disobedience, the
ejection from paradise into a universe of fear and dread.
Even the mark of Cain comes into the story, for the stripes
of the Tiger, we are told, will scar the first killer and his
descendants forever.

But the theme of expulsion from Eden runs like a *leit-
motif* through the whole of *The Jungle Books*. Mowgli, for
example, is thrust by accident out of the bosom of his family into the hard jungle, there to survive or not as chance
and his own talents may determine. The same is true of
Rikki-tikki-tavi, a mongoose who is washed away from his
parents in a summer flood and who must try to make a
place for himself in a new world, to find love and acceptance in a new and different society. Even such a story as
"The Miracle of Purun Bhagat," which is not about a child
and which seems at first glance to have little or nothing to
do with the other tales in *The Jungle Books*, does in fact
concern itself with the central theme of all these narratives.
For it deals with a man who leaves the life into which he
was born and enters upon a new and challenging existence.
Like Mowgli, Purun Bhagat is searching for the world to
which he truly belongs, and it is his discovery of that world
that is the old man's miracle.

Such self-discovery is as important to the philosophical
structure of the *bildungsroman* as is the motif of ejection
from paradise; the fashioning of the self out of suffering
and knowledge is the "development novel's" second crucial
theme, a theme which, in *The Jungle Books*, is given symbolic treatment by Kipling in a tale called "The White
Seal." This is the familiar "Messiah" story, told, to be sure,
with an unusual set of characters, but making the point
which all such stories make. Kotick's people are in bondage
to death at the hands of fur trappers. Everywhere he turns,

the white seal is told that nothing can be done about this fact. But he is a white seal; he is not like anybody else, he is only like himself. And so he steers always by his own reckoning, and when he at last releases his people from the threat of death, it is to find himself occupying on the new beach the position his father had occupied on the old. Mowgli, too, we have seen, must struggle with the reality of a world he never made (a reality which he learns to call "The Law"), in order, finally, to create himself. And the more he becomes uniquely himself, the more clearly he recognizes that he must return to his origins.

A good deal more might be said about *The Jungle Books* as *bildungsroman*. For our purposes, however, it is enough to point out that even as Kipling was undertaking what seems to be the "simple" task of writing animal stories for children, he was also, whether consciously or not, working in one of the more important literary genres of his day and doing his work with considerable originality. Indeed, this conscious or unconscious attempt of his to use what we are accustomed to thinking of as trivial or merely "entertaining" media for more serious themes is perhaps, while hardly shocking to audiences in an age of pop art, at the root of his persistent problem with educated readers. For in order to take Kipling seriously as an artist we must all too often abandon our expectations, not only our expectations of Rudyard Kipling the mustachioed jingoist but of the forms in which he frequently works—the beast epic, the fairy tale, the humorous dialect poem, the popular song, the entertaining anecdote, the ghost or horror story. More than most of his contemporaries, more, perhaps, than any other modern writer, Kipling used unlikely materials and techniques in his fiction as well as in his poetry. In an age when the rift between popular and serious literature was gradually widening from a gulf to an abyss he tried to build bridges which would unite the two shores. As a result, his best works will frequently be found to conceal surprisingly complex structures of meaning beneath their simple surfaces.

CHAPTER FOUR ▨

The Art of the Complex

i

If some readers have felt that Kipling was too simple-minded to be a serious artist, others have seen him as too cleverly complex, too devious, even, to be able to write poems and stories of any real quality; have condemned him, that is, for his willingness to sacrifice art not only to politics or journalism but also to a perverse preoccupation with craftsmanship for its own sake. Edward Wagenknecht, for example, in *The Cavalcade of the Novel*, characterizes Kipling as "the trickiest of all great writers,"[1] alluding to another of the charges most frequently leveled against the author,[2] that of being so fascinated by the "tricks" of the writing trade that he neglects the substance of his stories. "The mere machine of his art," says another critic, addressing himself to the same problem, "the gritty detachment of his style" give to too many of the poems and tales the appearance of being "things imposed from without"; his work, the critic continues, has very distinctly about it "the virtuosity of the Chinese juggler."[3]

---

1. Edward Wagenknecht, *Cavalcade of the English Novel* (New York, 1954), p. 402.

2. Henry Murray, for example, considered Kipling an "extremely clever man" rather than a poet or genius. See his *Robert Buchanan: A Critical Appreciation and Other Essays* (London, 1901), p. 161.

3. Boris Ford, "A Case for Kipling?" *The Importance of Scrutiny*, ed. Eric Bentley (New York, 1948), pp. 331, 325. Note that this accusation

To a certain extent, Kipling helped to establish this reputation for trickiness himself. He was fascinated by the pure
craft of writing, and in his posthumously published memoir, *Something of Myself*, he is at his best when he is
revelling in his "Chinese" virtuosity. About the story "Cold
Iron," for example, he writes with obvious pleasure:

> I worked the material in three or four overlaid tints and tex-
> tures, which might or might not reveal themselves, according
> to the shifting light of sex, youth and experience. It was like
> working lacquer and mother o' pearl, a natural combination,
> into the same scheme as niello and grisaille, and trying not to
> let the joins show.

Even the process of cutting a manuscript had its own mystique:

> Take of well-ground Indian ink as much as suffices and a camel-
> hair brush proportionate to the interspaces of your lines. In an
> auspicious hour, read your final draft and consider faithfully
> every paragraph, sentence and word, blacking out where req-
> uisite. . .

It is this relatively superficial preoccupation of Kipling's
with tools and techniques which has caused many critics
to question the writer's seriousness as an artist, especially
in his more difficult and puzzling works. Casual readers,
who know Kipling only through his jingly ballads and his
Just-So Stories, are always surprised to learn that the author of "How the Camel Got his Hump" is also the creator
of some of the most doggedly inexplicable fiction written
in the twentieth century. Indeed, the establishment of this

---

of trickiness, of self-conscious virtuosity, while apparently the reverse of
the attack we examined in the last chapter on Kipling's "little-brained"
ignorance of the rules of fiction, levels, like that attack, the charge of
superficiality.

fact has been one of the major contributions of recent Kipling criticism.[4] But because such works as "The Wish House," "Dayspring Mishandled," "The Gardener," and "Mrs. Bathurst"—to name only a few—are so abstruse, some commentators, brought up on the legend of Kipling's trickiness, can confront them only by assuming that they are not in earnest. One reader, for example, faced with the difficulties of "Mrs. Bathurst," and taking his cue from a remark made by Kipling in an entirely different context in *Something of Myself*, concluded his analysis of the work by dismissing it as a tale in which the author had "set out to write the worst story he could in order to hoax his readers."[5] Thus the accusation of trickiness is constantly being reinforced.

In the last analysis, however, what really matters is not whether Kipling was preoccupied with technique in his stories but whether he succeeded in making that technique serve the ends of his art. And to be able to come to some conclusion about this question, we need the sort of text which permits us to face squarely the issue which Wagenknecht raises. It should be an obviously serious work, one on which Kipling himself might have been willing to stake his reputation, and yet it should also be full of what can legitimately be called technical tricks. A story which clearly fits this description is "The Gardener." Its credentials are impressive; one critic, for example, has written of it: "I am not sure that it is not really the best story Kipling ever wrote."[6] On the other hand, it is pre-eminently a tale

---

4. See, among other works, J. M. S. Tompkins, *The Art of Rudyard Kipling* (London, 1959) and C. A. Bodelsen, *Aspects of Kipling's Art* (New York, 1964). The latter is particularly concerned with Kipling's "difficult" stories.

5. B. S. Browne, "The Unsolved Problem of 'Mrs. Bathurst,'" *Kipling Journal* (December 1959), 18.

6. Edmund Wilson, *The Wound and the Bow* (New York, 1947), p.

full of tricks and technique. Indeed, a critic bent on attacking the story could easily find at least three pointed and apparently very damaging questions to ask about it. First, he might inquire why Kipling introduces, at the end of what appears to be a fairly realistic story, an element of the supernatural. Next, he might well wonder why, in so brief a story as this, the author chooses to cover so many years and to crowd his pages with so much synopsis. And finally, he might ask why Kipling works so hard to conceal from his readers, through elaborate misdirection, the real circumstances of his narrative.

These three questions—and the last one in particular, with its oblique reference to the tale's O. Henry-like surprise ending—seem, merely by being raised, to make a strong presumptive case against "The Gardener" as a good story and an even stronger one against Kipling as a serious writer. On the other hand, it has long been considered one of the marks of Kipling's artistic skill that his most significant visions and many of his best works develop from his answers to such purely technical questions as those we have just asked. Edmund Wilson, for example, has commented that in "The Gardener," Kipling's "method of preparing a finale by concealing essential information in an apparently casual narrative produces an effect of tremendous power,"[7] and it is just this ability of Kipling's to generate power through the "mechanical" manipulation of characters and incidents which challenges Wagenknecht's unflattering portrait of the artist as a trickster fascinated with technical virtuosity for its own sake. Certainly, from the answers to these three questions a much less "tricky" and a much more serious Kipling emerges.

---

180. The presence of two negatives in this statement may serve to mitigate the compliment a little.

7. Wilson, p. 179.

ii

The first question, about supernatural elements in the tale, might best be dealt with against a background of other Kipling stories in which such elements appear. A list of these stories would be long and impressive, containing many of the author's best known works. It would include, among the earlier tales, "The Mark of the Beast," "At the End of the Passage," "The Phantom Rickshaw," "The Brushwood Boy," "The Bridge-Builders," "They," and "Wireless"; and among later ones, in addition to "The Gardener," "The Madonna of the Trenches," "Cold Iron," "Unprofessional," and "The Wish House." Kipling turned easily to the supernatural in his stories, seldom with any sense of strain or self-consciousness. Not that he was unaware of the problems involved in writing such tales. In "My Own True Ghost Story" he charmingly spoofs the more melodramatic and conventional elements of the genre, and he is not above implying supernatural doings in such a story as "The Return of Imray," and then of explaining everything rationally in the end. It is reasonable to assume, therefore, that when Kipling introduces supernatural occurrences into his stories, he does so not merely to thrill his readers or to get himself out of plot difficulties but rather to express an idea that he feels cannot be communicated in any other way.

Such an assumption does not come easily, however. Wilson, for example, having warmly praised "The Gardener" as the best of its author's tales, nevertheless feels constrained to add that the story "is not quite on the highest level," that Kipling "must still have his fairy-tale properties."[8] Thus he seems to associate the appearance of the supernatural in literature with some crucial failure of artis-

---

8. Wilson, p. 180.

tic will or imagination. As a theory, this seems unnecessarily limiting. To ask of a writer that he deal seriously with human beings as they really are is one thing. To insist that he handle this material in purely realistic terms is quite another. If the supernatural in literature is often the second-rate author's excuse for escaping from life into simple-minded or sentimental fantasy, it need not always be so abused. At its best—as Kipling uses it in "The Gardener," for example—the supernatural reinforces reality rather than distracting from it, represents the final intensification of the author's vision, too compressed and cryptic to find expression within the realistic framework of the rest of the tale, but itself ultimately expressive of reality.[9]

Kipling employs the supernatural at the end of "The Gardener" with restraint and precision. Indeed, the moment at which "The Gardener" moves beyond conventional reality is so unobtrusive that many readers at first fail to notice it. Yet the shock it provides intensifies and gives meaning to everything that has gone before, and all without itself usurping the central position. This last point is worth making. Most critical comments about "The Gardener" tend to emphasize the final incident at the expense of all the others. The incident is indeed an impressive one, but it is very briefly told and is unlike any other event in the story. Thus, while its compression and uniqueness give it its important function—to make clear what has gone before—the reader must not be distracted by this intensity into forgetting that it is what has gone before that is really the central matter of the story.

Any discussion of "what has gone before," however, re-

---

9. Elizabeth Bowen has said "I do not make use of the supernatural [in my short stories] as a get-out; it is inseparable (whether or not it comes to the surface) from my sense of life. That I feel it unethical—for some reason?—to allow the supernatural into a novel, may be one of my handicaps as a sincere novelist." *A Day in the Dark* (London, 1965), p. 9.

turns us to a consideration of synopsis in "The Gardener."
Present the facts of this tale to most writers of fiction, ask
them to compose a fifteen-page story based on those facts,
and, at least in the matter of structure, they would no doubt
all agree. Probably without exception they would open
their stories with Helen Turrell on her way to France to
visit the grave of her son, would incorporate necessary material by means of flashback, and would then return to the
present for the climactic scene in the cemetery. Indeed, it
would be surprising to find even one among all those
writers trying to crowd twenty years into fifteen pages by
beginning at the beginning and then proceeding doggedly
along to the end. Yet it is precisely this dogged but presumably calculated exposition which Kipling undertakes in
"The Gardener."

The question is why. We must assume that Kipling, a
deliberate craftsman, knew what he was doing when he
chose this particular structure for his story, and that therefore the ends he achieved with it were in fact the ends he
wanted to achieve. The most immediate effect of this organization is to give the story an ingenuous and casual air,
the air of being presented in a wholly unaccented way, free
from any artistic manipulation of the facts. This relaxed
and unclimactic quality of "The Gardener" contributes
significantly to the power of the final pages. Just as important, however, the apparently casual structuring of
material deliberately shifts our attention away from the
final scene, which in any case remains accented enough,
and focuses it instead where Kipling obviously wanted it to
be focused, on Helen's life in the village before she ever
dreamed of taking her trip, and even more specifically on
the village itself.

The very first sentence of "The Gardener," with its reference to what "everyone in the village knows," supports

this reading. From the purely technical point of view, Kipling had to present Helen's story second-hand to his readers if he wanted to play fair with them and yet continue to preserve his surprise, and this alone would have made it necessary for him to begin "The Gardener" with what the village knew rather than with what Helen knew. But this opening is more than just technically significant. Properly read it performs a thematic function as well, preparing us to learn later that it is what the village knows and what the village thinks that is the most important single fact in the lives of all the people in this story, and especially in the life of Helen Turrell. About Helen herself, the village knows what it has chosen to believe of Helen's own story.[10] But in a larger sense, Kipling says, what the village knows is what nearly every village has always "known" with calm certainty: that it is the chief guardian of public and private virtue and the defender of respectability; that it has the unquestioned duty and, through the enormous power of collective disapproval, the irresistible means of imposing upon its members, at whatever cost, its own way of life.

This may seem a harsh judgment, but the story insists upon it. The whole first paragraph is full of smug self-satisfaction. "Everyone in the village knew that Helen Turrell did her duty," that her brother George "had tried his family severely since early youth," that he had "entangled himself" with the daughter of a retired non-commissioned officer, and that Helen had "nobly" taken charge, though she was thirty-five and "independent" (the official euphemism for "unmarried"), and might well "have washed her hands of the whole disgraceful affair." Every phrase

10. In a similar situation in George Moore's *Esther Waters*, Esther is advised to "give herself out as Jackie's [her son's] aunt. 'None believes them stories, but they make one feel respectable like.' "

is a self-righteous judgment, a complacent formula that we can imagine being passed along from one group of gossips to the next. Indeed, the statement that George Turrell "had tried his family severely since early youth" might well preserve the very wording of his disappointed parents' own complaints. And when we read, in a sharply ironic statement that is clearly the consensus of the village, that "mercifully, George's father and mother were both dead," we are obliged to share Kipling's pity and contempt for people who prefer death to disapproval. The baleful influence of respectability, then, is Kipling's theme in "The Gardener," and in Helen Turrell he portrays a woman who has been defeated by a repressive, parochial society and whose only chance of salvation lies in the hope of an act of grace which she is destined not to understand when it comes.

The days pass slowly for Helen in the story, the flat, chronological ordering of incidents in the narrative contributing to our sense of the wearing, uneventful process of life. We can imagine them passing in the same way for her in her youth with her parents still alive and she not yet a spinster. Indeed, the story offers a number of clues to the incidents of these early days; the departure of her brother, the death of her mother and father, her thirty-fifth birthday, the impetuous, bungled love affair, so peripheral to her real life that no trace of the lover remains except in the curve of Michael's mouth, the trip to the south of France, the concocting of the story, the return home and the beginning of the elaborate game of cat and mouse.

Nor, Kipling means us to see, could any of this have been avoided. For given the village as it is and given Helen as she is, the outcome is inevitable. But both are required, the village with its implacable rules of propriety, ready at every moment to withhold approval, and Helen greatly in need of that approval. It is a curiously corrupting conspiracy, one in which oppressors and victims are indistinguishable, in which a villager may at one moment be the object of community pressure and the next may himself join the group to stamp out vitality somewhere else. Kipling makes this point most insistently when he has Helen, so often the victim in this story, momentarily assuming for Mrs. Scarsworth the role of community conscience and offering, in response to the woman's agonized outburst, not the understanding and compassion which her own experience should have made possible, but instead, a repellent, conventional gesture.

The inability to feel or to acknowledge feeling is one of the prices the villagers must pay for their system. By the time news of Michael's death reaches home, for example, the village is old in experience of war and has "evolved a ritual to meet it," a ritual based upon the repression of feeling. The emotional blankness of the response is what is most striking about it. "When the postmistress handed her seven-year-old daughter the official telegram to·take to Miss Turrell, she observed to the Rector's gardener: 'It's Miss Helen's turn now.' He replied, thinking of his own son: 'Well, he's lasted longer than some.'" Edmund Wilson is quite right when he notes that in "The Gardener," Kipling "pities now rather than boasts about the self-disciplined and much-enduring British,"[11] but he would have been fairer to point out that Kipling had never anywhere in his work boasted of a self-discipline which dries up the soul. As if to underline the emotional bankruptcy of the village adults, the telegram scene continues for another moment, following the little delivery girl as she weeps "aloud, because Master Michael had often given her sweets." At seven, the child has not yet been touched

---

11. Wilson, p. 180.

by the village and its ways. Perhaps she will be one of the
few villagers lucky enough to "try her family severely," as
Helen's brother had done, and to leave one day for the
other side of the world. (There are two sides to everything.) More likely, however, the village will become for
her, as it has become for Helen, the only world there is,
will require of her the sort of allegiance that has driven
Helen to be untrue to herself, to deny her love and renounce her son.

More than just Helen Turrell's story, however, "The
Gardener" broadens its horizon in the course of the narrative to emphasize the universality of the themes of repression and self-betrayal. It is in France, for example, in the
tar-paper shed of a Commissioner of Graves, that Helen
meets the Lancashire woman, whose case is so much like
her own. The woman, talking to the Commissioner, reveals
that she is searching for her son whose "proper name was
Anderson, but [who], coming of respectable folk, had of
course enlisted under the name of Smith," and from what
we have already learned about villages and their attitudes
toward non-commissioned officers, the story seems painfully authentic. Like Helen, the Lancashire woman has
been separated from her child by an exaggerated and destructive commitment to respectability. Moreover, searching as she is for her son named Smith, her son with more
than one Christian name who seems to have fallen on more
than one battlefield, she becomes a symbol of all mothers
who have lost their children through their own false values
and have afterwards sought for them in vain.

Helen leaves the tar-paper shed and goes for tea to a
mauve and blue striped wooden structure, described as
having a "false front." Here she meets a woman named
Mrs. Scarsworth who, like herself, has been living a lie for
many years, terrified of what people might think of the

truth. The difference between Helen and Mrs. Scarsworth, however, is that the latter has followed her lie as far as it will take her and now recognizes the need for something more. In an emotional outburst of the sort which Helen would be incapable of, she confesses her secret, hoping in this way to ease her pain. But that ease does not come. Mrs. Scarsworth has been too steeped in dishonesty for too long and she is dishonest even in her moment of truth. She confesses to a stranger when it is to the people of her "village" that she must speak if she wishes to free herself from the curse of respectability. And even at the instant of confession she still sees the great experience of her life—"the one real thing"—through the reproving eyes of the community. " 'He was everything to me that he *oughtn't to have been* ' " (italics mine), she says, negating the whole purpose of her outburst. Under the circumstances, Helen can hardly do anything but what she does. She has been invited to take the part of the village and to cast the fallen woman out, and she accomplishes her task with the terrible banality of her reply. "My dear, my dear," she says. "Mrs. Scarsworth stepped back, her face all mottled. 'My God!' said she. 'Is *that* how you take it?' Helen could not speak, and the woman went out."

The character of Mrs. Scarsworth contributes to the story in many ways. First, it permits Kipling to explore the psychology of a woman who has sinned against the social code and who, in attempting to conceal her guilt, has condemned herself to a greater punishment than any which society could have imposed. Mrs. Scarsworth's position is precisely Helen Turrell's, but the author could not have discussed these matters in terms of Helen without prematurely giving away the secret of the story. Second, the relationship that develops between the two women grows into a kind of metaphor for the conventionality of their

G

lives. Meeting over tea in a structure with a false front, they speak of hotel accommodations and Kodak snapshots of graves. Yet even when the passion that is consuming both of them breaks through the reserve, it can find no words to express itself, for the village has never taught the two women the language of reality. Mrs. Scarsworth's horrified retreat represents, at least in part, the woman's recognition that she will never be able to escape from the prison of banality to which she has condemned herself. And it is this recognition which is her third contribution to the story. For having tried and failed to resolve her problem in human terms, she has prepared the reader to see that only a more-than-human act of grace can ever hope to comfort such human beings as these who lack even the vocabulary of feeling.

Thus far we have seen how the arrangement of material in "The Gardener" has tended to focus our attention on the village and all that the village represents—the suppression, in the name of propriety and self-discipline, of human feeling. This same synopsis of incidents, however—chronological and unaccented—performs still another and equally significant function in the tale. It underlines the fact that the bereaved Helen Turrell, the woman we meet searching for her son in France, is the end product of a long, slow process, a process which, over many years and in a thousand unspectacular ways, has shaped her into the person she has become. And it is essential that we recognize how successful this process has been and how irreversible it is if we are to understand why no human solace can really touch Helen any more; if we are to appreciate, that is, why only an act of grace can even momentarily break through her carefully acquired reserve.

The need to understand the process by which a woman like Helen Turrell is created was obviously as important to

Kipling as his desire to understand the woman herself. Thus, one of the central metaphors of this story invokes such a process. The news of Michael's death has just reached the young man's mother, the round of condolence visits has begun, and Helen remembers that once, on one of her son's leaves, "he had taken her over a munition factory, where she saw the progress of a shell from blank-iron to the all but finished article. It struck her at the time that the wretched thing was never left alone for a single second, and 'I'm being manufactured[12] into a bereaved next of kin,' she told herself, as she prepared her documents."

The passage is a significant one because the process of manufacturing which Helen here describes is identical with the one which has been going on all her life. From the moment she submitted herself to the discipline of her village, voluntarily making her life "public property," she too has never been left alone for a single second. She too was blank-iron once, like the little girl who delivered the telegram, and is now an all but finished article. Nor is her bereavement really a recent phenomenon, for no one is more surely a bereaved next of kin than a mother who has never been allowed to acknowledge her own son. Thus, the woman who sets out at the end of "The Gardener" to find her son's grave is beyond ordinary assistance; the quest she has undertaken in the forlorn hope of recovering an old love buried years before is one in which neither the man in the tar-paper shack nor Mrs. Scarsworth can be of any help. With the useless paper of directions held tightly in her hand, Helen stands alone amid "a waist-high wilderness" of crosses, and moves "to the left and the right hope-

---

12.   The phrase also appears earlier in the story where Michael's battalion is described as having led a "meretorious and unexacting life, while the Somme was being manufactured."

lessly wondering by what guidance she [shall] ever come to her own."

It is at this moment, with revelation at hand for both Helen and the reader, that we are ready to consider the ironic, inverted form into which Kipling chose to cast "The Gardener." The technique of deliberate concealment is one we meet with often in Kipling's fiction. In "Mrs. Bathurst," for example, the carefully contrived obscurity of the narrative is deliberately designed to entice readers into searching for meaning in the tale and thus into actually participating in the theme of the story—man's eternal quest for knowledge and control and his permanent inability to achieve either. In the same way, the concealment which characterizes the presentation of "The Gardener" echoes the theme of concealment in the story itself and prepares the reader to experience the same shock that Helen does at the end, the same almost physical blow of surprise and insight. At the very moment that the word "son" is spoken by the gardener, releasing for an instant in Helen the repressed emotions of a lifetime, it also releases in the reader a sudden and parallel burst of understanding through which he can actually feel as well as apprehend the experience Helen is having.

Kipling obviously had to be careful in preparing for this effect. The moment of surprise in a story like this can easily become a distraction if the reader entertains even for a moment the notion that the author has not been playing fair with him. Thus at the end of "The Gardener," Kipling sees to it that our sense of shock is mingled with a corresponding sense of inevitability. He does this by introducing, in the course of the story, incidents and images which, too subtle themselves to give the surprise away, nevertheless subliminally prepare the reader for the revelation that is to come. The heavy irony of the first paragraph, already suggestive on a first reading, contributes its bit. The hint of secrecy and suppression in Michael's background prepares the reader still further. The episode with Mrs. Scarsworth goes almost too far but catches itself in time, attention being cleverly focused on the woman, her camera and her commissions, and away from Helen.

Perhaps most explicit of all is the almost symbolic description of Michael's death. In it we learn that, a shell splinter having killed the young man at once, "the next shell uprooted and laid down over the body what had been the foundation of a barn wall, so neatly that none but an expert would have guessed that anything unpleasant had happened." Here the themes of concealment and burial coincide, the one being made synonymous with the other, so that very deliberately we are prepared to see that Helen's search for Michael's grave is also a search for the burial-place of her own hidden life. "Are you sure you know your grave?" says the man in the tar-paper shack. "It makes such a difference." Even the word "unpleasant" in the passage seems to suggest the concealment of a social mistake rather than the burial of a man.

The appearance of the figure of Jesus at the end of the story is also prepared for with some subtlety. The resurrection of Michael from his makeshift grave is one clue. The statement that Helen felt "the agony of being waked up to a second life," and the fact that the trip to France is taking place at Easter time also help to set the stage for the last scene. And of course any reader familiar with the New Testament will recognize, at the end of Kipling's tale, the suggestion of the scene in John 20.11-16 in which Mary Magdalene comes to Christ's tomb only to find the stone rolled away and the sepulchre empty, and turning to Jesus standing behind her, "supposing him to be the gardener," asks to know where her Lord has been taken for burial.

At the equivalent point in Kipling's story Helen Turrell has a similar experience. As she wanders helplessly in a "merciless sea of black crosses," among black graves not yet planted out, in which she can "distinguish no order or arrangement," she is powerless, alone, to come to her goal, nor would another human being be of any use. Human understanding cannot help her; we have seen how it failed to help Mrs. Scarsworth. It is not someone to hear her confession that she needs, but rather someone who will understand everything without confession. In the end the need is simply supplied. The gardener, speaking the word "son," for a moment bestows on Helen her motherhood again, and shows her the way to the grave she is seeking. In the words of the epigraph, "for one day in all the years . . . the stone is rolled away." Even so, the story closes on a final note of irony. All through "The Gardener" it is Helen who has known the truth and the reader who has been in the dark. But in the last line of the tale the positions are reversed. The readers all know the identity of the strange man in the cemetery. Only Helen goes away "supposing him to be the gardener."

To the three questions that might be raised by critics about the presumed trickiness of "The Gardener," then, it has been possible to respond with a single answer. If by "trickiness" is meant indulgence in mere virtuoso effects for their own sake, Kipling is no trickster. For though his tale is certainly a triumph of technical facility, technique in the story is, as we have seen, always at the service of theme; indeed, the theme of "The Gardener" itself represents an insight into the uselessness of trickery, into the futility of life lived on any terms but its own. This fact may surprise readers who associate Kipling with certain stereotyped positions: the sanctity of the British Empire, the importance of playing the game, and so on. For in the story, the author neither condemns nor approves of his characters on the purely superficial grounds of conventional morality. On the one hand, he does not, in "The Gardener," become sentimental about Helen Turrell and her quest. Compare his restraint with Fitzgerald's lack of it in the scene from *Tender Is The Night* in which Dick Diver and some friends, dining soon after a trip to a battle field cemetery, notice some women sitting at a nearby table.

An instinct made Dick suck back the grave derision that formed on his tongue; he asked the waiter to find out who they were.

"Those are the gold-star muzzers," explained the waiter.

Aloud and in low voices they exclaimed. Rosemary's eyes filled with tears.

"Probably the young ones are the wives," said Nicole.

Over his wine Dick looked at them again; in their happy faces, the dignity that surrounded and pervaded the party, he perceived all the maturity of an older America. For a while the sobered women who had come to mourn for their dead, for something they could not repair, made the room beautiful.

Kipling does not deal in such sentimentality. On the other hand, he does not dogmatically hold his characters to a rigid code of conduct, nor does he descend to the level of jingoistic patriotism, for he sees that these things—sentimentality, rigidity, jingoism—are the real trickery, in life as well as in art. In the world of "The Gardener," what is important is that life should have value, to quote Lionel Trilling's essay on Kipling, "outside the notions of orderliness, success, and gentility."[13] Thus, the only judgment which the story recognizes as significant is the judgment which life passes on itself, a judgment against which no trickery can prevail.

---

13. Lionel Trilling, "Kipling," *The Liberal Imagination* (New York, 1950), p. 123.

iii

Kipling's "trickiness" in "The Gardener" consists, in general, of his display of technical virtuosity, and, in particular, of his withholding, until the very end of the story, of the truth about Helen Turrell's relationship to the boy she brings up as her nephew. Once the nature of that relationship is understood, however, the tale presents no further difficulties. That is to say, if "The Gardener" may properly be included among Kipling's puzzling stories, it is at any rate a tale whose puzzle is wholly cleared up by the last page. The author wrote many other stories, however, which are puzzling—and so, by implication, tricky—in ways that "The Gardener" is not. Tales like "The Dog Hervey," for example, and "Mrs. Bathurst" are so elusive, so astonishingly reticent in their structures and syntax, as well as in their subject matter, that their very existence constitutes a puzzle which seems forever beyond solution. C. S. Lewis has spoken of "Mrs. Bathurst" as being "so compressed that in the completed version it is not quite told."[14] The allusion here is to the Kipling method of manuscript cutting with brush and Indian ink. Lewis is suggesting that the momentum of pruning "Mrs. Bathurst" may have carried Kipling, all unaware, past the point of intelligibility; that the obscurity of the story must be laid to the author's unfortunate preoccupation with technique.

Other critics, attempting to account for the inscrutability of "Mrs. Bathurst," have pointed to the delight which Kipling often took in puzzling his readers just for the sake of the puzzle; the author was always, in one way or another, propounding riddles and offering for their solutions artfully inadequate clues. Even in his posthumous auto-

14   C. S. Lewis, "Kipling's World," *They Asked for a Paper* (London, 1962), p. 73.

biographical sketch, *Something of Myself*, he continued adding to these mysteries, alluding at one point to a code hidden in his story "Cold Iron," a code for which, he insisted, he himself had forgotten the key.[15] Elsewhere in the memoir he mentions a factual error which had slipped into one of his works, and then for no particular reason he fails to identify the work. As a result, Kipling scholars have been trying ever since to discover the notorious error, although, in fact, the author had through the years made and admitted to many such mistakes.

Kipling's preoccupation with puzzles and mysteries, it has been suggested, was a result of his lifelong need to be, and to prove himself to be, an insider. The function of an insider—perhaps his most important function—is to keep everyone who is not on the inside out, and such exclusiveness is traditionally maintained through the use of secret and carefully guarded rituals, everything from special handshakes and cryptic jargon to ceremonies of almost Byzantine complexity. Kipling loved dialects, at least in part for the sense of belonging they gave him, loved to learn the shop talk of the professionals and to use it, without glossaries, in his stories and poems. He was attracted to the Masons no doubt as much by their secrecy and ritual as by their cult of craftsmanship. And as we watch the old Kipling, the old recluse, strewing his memoir with the puzzles, the mysteries, the veiled hints he delighted in so much, we can almost see him moving toward that perfect exclusiveness and ultimate safety for which all insiders secretly yearn—the club of one.

Recognizing this truth about Kipling, we would nevertheless be wrong if we were to dismiss the obscure and puzzling style of a story like "Mrs. Bathurst" as just another

---

15. It has been suggested that the italicized words in this story, extracted and rearranged, offer a comment on the theme.

hoax, just another instance of the author's trickiness. The convoluted later style may indeed have received its initial impulse from that same emotional unsteadiness which produced the puzzles and the cryptograms. But Kipling was an artist, and like any artist he knew the secret of converting what were weaknesses in himself into strengths in his art. Thus, what is most significant about "Mrs. Bathurst" is the fact that, compressed and cryptic as it may be, nothing essential is omitted. Indeed, Kipling's struggle for compression and his pruning away of representational elements in "Mrs. Bathurst" to permit concentration on other values justifies the closest possible reading of the text and makes the critic responsible not only for clarifying the surface action of the story but also for discovering the significance of that action. What a detailed study of "Mrs. Bathurst" reveals is a powerful tale embodying Kipling's characteristically bleak vision of life and composed in a style far enough ahead of its time to account for the story's reputation as a perennial puzzler.

The first great stumbling block for readers of "Mrs. Bathurst" is the story's peculiar structure. Accustomed, in conventional tales, to a series of scenes all dealing more or less with the same people and all developing more or less logically from one another—as scenes do, for example, in the usual motion picture—readers are confused by a story which is constructed instead along the lines of a newsreel. For on a first reading, the scenes in this story, like those in a newsreel, seem to have only the most casual connection with one another. They begin and end abruptly and, so it appears, arbitrarily, and they deal with a number of different people and situations without at first seeming to coalesce into a single story. It is this random and accidental quality of "Mrs. Bathurst" which led critics to suggest that Kipling had cut too much. But given Kipling's intense awareness of what he was doing it might be more profitable to follow one of J. M. S. Tompkins' suggestions and accept the apparently confused structure of "Mrs. Bathurst" as a deliberate part of the author's plan and as the first important fact we have about the story.[16] If it is not immediately plain how this fact contributes to the expression of the story's theme, we can turn to one of the narrative's central incidents for clarification.

The comparison of "Mrs. Bathurst" to a newsreel is not an arbitrary one. In the early nineteen-hundreds, when pictures that actually moved were still a novelty, Kipling cleverly designed his tale to turn on the showing of a film and included a detailed description of a newsreel, or rather a collection of random movie scenes, in his story. Barwick Browne has written that Kipling allowed himself to become overly absorbed by the cinematograph in "Mrs. Bathurst," thus losing control of the rest of his narrative.[17] But Kipling's reaction to the phenomenon of the motion picture was not the delight of a child with a new toy, but rather the fascination of an artist with a new metaphor. The moving picture show carefully described in "Mrs. Bathurst" is, the reader is meant to see, a metaphor for life. It is an accidental grouping of scenes—"London Bridge with the omnibuses—a troopship goin' to the war—marines on parade at Portsmouth, an' the Plymouth Express arrivin' at Paddin'-ton;" scenes which are, according to Pyecroft, "the real thing—alive an' movin'," and which, together with the apparently random structure of the story, serve to express what is the central theme of "Mrs. Bathurst"—the fortuitousness of life.

---

16.   J. M. S. Tompkins, *The Art of Rudyard Kipling* (London, 1959), p. 89.

17.   Barwick Browne, "What Happened in 'Mrs. Bathurst?' " *Kipling Journal* (July 1949), 10.

This theme runs through all of Kipling's work and accounts, in part, for his pragmatism and for his refusal, so annoying at times, to take the "long view." His world, we have seen, is a chaotic place, ruled, as far as any man can tell, by blind chance. Sooner or later everyone comes to trial and must struggle to extract some order from the chaos, to impose on the universe some law, useful at least to himself. At the crucial moment, Hooper says, a man "goes crazy—or just saves himself;" that is, he either echoes the disorder of the universe with the disorder of his own mind, or else, through his own efforts, he somehow manages to organize at least one corner of the chaos so that he can go on living. "Mrs. Bathurst" is the story of "Click" Vickery's trial in life and of his failure.

There is a good deal more in "Mrs. Bathurst," however, beyond the newsreel itself and the newsreel-like structure of the story, to support Kipling's theme of the accidentalness of life. The narrative opens with an error. "The day that I chose to visit H. M. S. *Peridot* in Simon's Bay," we are told at the outset, "was the day that the Admiral had chosen to send her up the coast. She was just steaming out to sea as my train came in." Having thus made a long trip out of his way for nothing, the narrator is next involved in a more pleasant accident. He has "the luck to come across" his friend Inspector Hooper, and the two men go off to Hooper's railroad car office at the mouth of False Bay where they are shortly joined by Pyecroft and Pritchard, who are themselves only in the neighborhood by chance, their ship having unexpectedly put into drydock for overhaul. At this point Kipling has spent three pages getting his four conversationalists together by a series of mistakes and coincidences when he might just as easily have opened the story with the four already gathered. The emphasis upon accident is inescapable.

This emphasis continues. We are told in passing, for example, that the Bass beer which Sergeant Pritchard contributes to the refreshment has been thrown over the wall to him by a woman who mistook him for someone else. A few moments later we find Pritchard himself mistakenly assuming that Hooper is a police officer. Still later we learn that Vickery's improperly fitted dental plate was made to replace the teeth he'd lost in an accident with an ammunition hoist. And perhaps most suggestive of all, the fateful appearance of Mrs. Bathurst on the movie screen is immediately preceded and, so to speak, introduced by the quite gratuitous image of "an old man with a rug 'oo'd dropped a book an' was tryin' to pick it up."

In addition to all these incidents, however, there remain two passages in "Mrs. Bathurst" which state even more directly the central theme. One is the strange episode of Boy Niven and the other is a short dramatic scene which serves the story as an epigraph. The Boy Niven scene, presented in great detail, seems at first glance to have no connection at all with the rest of the action. This fact has inspired at least one commentator to make the suggestion, already alluded to, that in "Mrs. Bathurst," Kipling had deliberately set out to write the worst story he could in order to hoax his readers, and that the episode of Boy Niven was inserted as a metaphorical warning to those who might otherwise be led astray. This theory is, of course, based on the assumption that the tale of Boy Niven has nothing to do with the rest of "Mrs. Bathurst." In fact, it has a great deal to do with it.

It is Pyecroft who tells the story. Boy Niven, who "said he was born at the back o' Vancouver Island, and *all* the time the beggar was a balmy Barnado Orphan," lures eight sailors, among them Pyecroft and Pritchard, away from their duties one day with a wholly fictitious tale about a generous uncle and free land. For twenty-four hours he leads the sailors on a meaningless, random trek over an uninhabited and uninhabitable island in the Vancouver Archipelago. Finally, a search party sent out for the eight catches up with them and returns them, in disgrace, to their ship where, as a last indignity, *they* are accused of having led the *boy* astray.

This episode, compounded of mistaken identity, misinformation, random wandering and errors in judgment, is, like the cinema, a metaphor for the story's general theme. In addition, however, it strikingly illuminates specific details of the action to follow. The desertion of the eight sailors, for example, foreshadows Vickery's own behavior. Desertion of duty may be considered the first act in the abandonment of order, and Vickery is presented to us throughout the story as a deserter, one who buckles under the pressure of accident. A family man who displays photographs of his daughter, he deserts his duty to his family when he becomes infatuated with Mrs. Bathurst. Soon, however, he deserts her too, and when we meet him he is guilt-ridden and on the point of deserting his naval duties to begin the rootless life of a tramp. The consequence of such a life of desertion, the Boy Niven story suggests, is a kind of madness, an aimless wandering of the sort that Vickery indulges in each night after the picture show, and will continue to indulge in as a tramp up-country until he achieves, during an electrical storm, the ultimate disorganization of death. And it is no doubt more than coincidence that when Hooper asks Pyecroft what punishment the eight sailors had received for deserting and following Boy Niven, Pyecroft replies picturesquely, "Heavy thunder with continuous lightning. . . ."

The epigraph of "Mrs. Bathurst" establishes this same theme in a brief, highly compressed dramatic scene composed in Kipling's best Elizabethan or Jacobean style.[18] The scene takes place in what just the day before had been a great city, but what is now only a sacked ruin, so fickly has fortune bestowed and withdrawn its favor. Three men are discussing together an unfortunate groom who, in the face of totally disinterested gods, has just been hanged, leaving his soul to pluck "the left sleeve of Destiny in Hell to overtake why she clapped him up like a fly on a sunny wall." The indifference of the universe does not even offer the man the poor consolation of knowing who is to blame for his destruction.

She that damned him to death knew not that she did it, or she would have died ere she had done it. For she loved him. He that hangs him does so in obedience to the Duke, and asks no more than "Where is the rope?" The Duke, very exactly he hath told us, works God's will, in which holy employ he's not to be questioned.

This inability to apportion blame correctly follows necessarily from the fortuitousness of life. The problem appears in the Boy Niven episode as well as in the epigraph and has its counterpart in the rest of the story. Pyecroft is extremely indignant when he tells of how he and his seven colleagues were held responsible for what Boy Niven had done to them. But when he comes to discuss Vickery, his values seem strangely reversed. Vickery's obvious helplessness in the face of his infatuation makes him at least as much a victim of Mrs. Bathurst as the eight sailors ever were of the "Boy," but Pyecroft and Pritchard, especially the latter, are almost vehement in their exoneration of the woman. Their confusion, like that of the groom, "baited on all sides by Fortune," is understandable, for men who

---

18. See Ann M. Weygandt, *Kipling's Reading* (Philadelphia, 1939), p. 40 for a discussion of Kipling's efforts in this vein.

believe that the principle of cause and effect operates the world instinctively try to fix responsibility somewhere. But in a world whose guiding principle is accident, responsibility loses all meaning, and coincidence, no longer just the crude expedient of a lazy artist, becomes the mechanism that blindly runs the world. The last we see of the condemned groom, the gods, in their infinite arbitrariness, are destroying him with the same "long-stored lightnings loosed yesterday 'gainst some King."

The theme of the intransigence of the universe is established beyond any doubt in "Mrs. Bathurst." But in the story, Vickery does not come up against some vague and generalized aspect of that intransigence; he confronts, in the widow from Aukland, a particular manifestation of it. In the epigraph, we leave the miserable groom "railing at fortune and woman's love," and it is woman's love that is the special aspect of chaos that destroys Vickery. Kipling's attitude toward woman is idiosyncratic.[19] Women as individuals may be charming and wholly innocent and yet at the same time may be acting, unconsciously, as the agents of a terrible power totally beyond their understanding or control. And though this power may originally have been generated by some overwhelming creative urge, its random, mindless application can just as easily be deadly and destructive.

This blind application of power by women is illustrated in "Mrs. Bathurst" in a number of ways. "She that damned him to death knew not that she did it," says the epigraph

19. In an article in the *Kipling Journal* (July 1930), 10, Basil M. Bazely discusses a Kipling female type, the woman who destroys a man without knowing she has done it or why it has happened. In this connection he quotes from "The Vampire": "Belong to the woman who did not know/ (And now we know that she never could know)/ And did not understand!" See also the woman in "Wressley of the Foreign Office" and Maisie in *The Light That Failed*.

in a phrase that might well stand alone as the motto of the story. Pritchard's bottle of beer is tossed to him by a woman whose charms begin to work automatically the moment she sees a man, even though he happens to be the wrong one. In fact, so automatic is female attractiveness that Pyecroft, concluding his terrible, cautionary story of Vickery's degradation, does not hesitate to break off the narrative for a moment to glance idly out the door and remark, "Pretty girl under that Kapje."

Mrs. Bathurst herself is the most important of these symbols of women's blind power. She is, in person, a charming woman and innocent of any destructive designs on any man. Yet so great is her attractive power, of which she is only the unconscious vessel, that men who meet her once can never forget her. She has, in a word that Kipling used before Hollywood did, "It." "Tisn't beauty, so to speak," says Pyecroft, "nor good talk necessarily. It's just It." Pritchard reverently tells of his encounters with the lady, of how she fascinated him—she enormously flattered men by remembering them over long intervals—and he mentions in passing how she would glance up flirtatiously at him from under her eyebrows "in that blindish way she had o' lookin'. . . ." Later Mrs. Bathurst is again described as looking "blindish" as she comes forward out of the movie screen toward the audience in the cinema. The word is not repeated idly. Mrs. Bathurst, at the moment of her greatest influence, is acting most blindly, most devotedly as an agent of a blind universe. "She that damned him to death knew not that she did it." It is in her capacity as an indifferent Fortune that her name gives the title to the story.

iv

It would be useful for us, at this point, to consider what it is that happens in "Mrs. Bathurst." A warrant

H

officer named Vickery, within eighteen months of his
pension, has deserted his duty under peculiar circumstances in the back country of South Africa. Four men
gather by chance in a railroad car and after some rambling
discussion undertake to piece together Vickery's story from
the fragments that each of them has. It seems that Vickery
was a devoted family man until the day he met and fell in
love with the fascinating Mrs. Bathurst, a widow who ran
a small hotel for sailors in New Zealand. Many sailors,
among them married ones, have casual affairs with women
—Pyecroft and Pritchard have had more than they can
remember—but Vickery, described somewhat ironically as
a superior man, has apparently fallen deeply under Mrs.
Bathurst's irresistible spell. And if the epigraph is to be
taken as shedding any light on the story, the phrase "for
she loved him" suggests that Mrs. Bathurst was equally
serious. At any rate, Pyecroft says, "There must 'ave been
a good deal between 'em, to my way o' thinkin'." The epigraph also suggests, in astrological terms, the passionate
nature of the relationship, speaking as it does of "Venus,
when Vulcan caught her with Mars in the house of stink-
ing Capricorn." (Vulcan is, of course, the classical artificer
of lightning bolts.)

What the exact nature of that "good deal between 'em"
was we are never certain, and there are those who feel that
Kipling was wrong to apply his technique of calculated
obscurity, which we shall see was quite valid elsewhere, to
the story's central relationship. Information about Vickery
and Mrs. Bathurst, the argument runs, is no substitute for
a picture of the two of them together, for a confrontation
that might have drawn the reader more personally into the
story, engaged his sympathy, illuminated Vickery's fate
and made it more poignant. It is difficult to defend Kipling
and his reticence on this point, but mistaken or not he

chose to keep the germinal experience of his story on the very edges of the narrative and to make us struggle to discover even the few facts he thought it necessary for us to have: that Vickery met Mrs. Bathurst, that his life became deeply entangled with hers so that to put his affairs in order would have taken more courage and strength than he had in the world, and that in the end he deserted her.

From that time, apparently, from that failure, dates the beginning of the madness which Pyecroft says must have been going on for years and which characterizes Vickery's last months. But the madness does not reach a crisis until Vickery attends a moving picture show one night in Cape Town and sees Mrs. Bathurst walking out of the screen toward him. We can imagine how he must have felt at the sight. The pictures, we are told, were extremely lifelike— "just like life"—and so realistic that when an engine headed straight at the audience, the ladies in the first row of the theatre jumped. To Vickery, burdened with his guilt, that enormous figure of Mrs. Bathurst bearing "blindishly" down on him must have been terrifying. Perhaps it made him think of a grim and now far-off domestic scene, the long-feared confrontation of husband, wife and lover to which that detraining had led. Perhaps, on the other hand, there had been no confrontation at all. Kipling does not offer enough information for us to be certain about what happened in London, and we can only conclude that he did not think it important for his readers to know the details; the merest suggestion of disaster was enough. The details he did want his readers to have however, he made extraordinarily graphic: the looming figures on the cinema screen, Vickery's guilty terror, and the chance fact that Mrs. Bathurst, hurrying one day from a railroad car, blundered blindly and unwittingly into range of a camera and thus was made the accidental tool of fortune, damning

Vickery to death from thousands of miles away and never knowing she had done it. Hence the irony in Pritchard's repeated, almost panicky requests for assurance, "Say what you please, Pye, but you don't make me believe it was any of 'er fault."

The effect of the motion picture—ironically titled "Home and Friends"—on Vickery is overwhelming and complex. On the one hand it awakens again all of his passionate infatuation for Mrs. Bathurst, drawing him back to the show night after night and leaving him, at the end of each performance, counting the minutes till the next. On the other hand it intensifies his sense of guilt and of inadequacy and contributes further to the disorder that will in the end destroy him. This effect manifests itself physically in Vickery's mad wanderings over Cape Town and in his suicidal urge, once the movie has completed its run and is about to move on, to abandon his duty and follow the film up-country.

What he says to the captain to win release from duty we are not told. All we know is that the two men speak for an hour, that Vickery comes away from the meeting in good spirits, and that the captain emerges a moment later shipping his courtmartial face, a face he had last worn on the day some of his men had dumped the ship's gunsights overboard. It is significant that gunsights, like the gyroscope mentioned earlier in the story as having been deliberately damaged, are instruments designed to keep men on target and on course, and as such are absolutely indispensable aboard a war ship. The captain thus reacts to indications of instability in one of his officers as he had done once before to the deliberate destruction of essential guidance equipment. It also is significant that in the description of the ship during Vickery's interview with the captain, there appear in the space of seven lines the words "execution of 'is duty," "my lawful occasions," "as a general rule," and "my duties," all emphasizing that ordered aspect of navy life which Vickery's madness is forcing him to flee. In the end, he is ordered off by himself on special assignment to Bloemfontein, an assignment from which he will never return.

Just before he leaves he encounters Pyecroft for the last time and tries to unburden himself a little of his guilt. "I've one thing to say before shakin' 'ands," Pyecroft recalls his words. "Remember that I am *not* a murderer, because my lawful wife died in childbed six weeks after I came out. That much at least I am clear of." This is a cryptic speech but it comes a little more into focus when we realize that Kipling restored the word "childbed" to the passage when he was preparing the magazine version of the story for book publication.[20] Vickery clearly feels responsible for his wife's death—elsewhere he speaks of himself as capable of murder—and physically, of course, he *is* responsible. His real guilt, however, has to do with his sense of having killed her by betraying her with Mrs. Bathurst. Furthermore, there is the sense of having, in his weakness, betrayed Mrs. Bathurst with his wife. This compound treachery leads to such self-loathing that, like the groom in the epigraph, Vickery "must e'en die now to live with myself one day longer." Certainly he desires nothing more, in his weari-

---

20. Professor C. A. Bodelsen has collated the two texts and accounts for the differences between them by suggesting that the magazine version was rigorously censored "to eliminate all references to human reproduction." *Aspects of Kipling's Art*, p. 151. An alternate explanation of this line is that Vickery knows Mrs. Bathurst has died (hence his fascination with her nightly revivals on the movie screen), and feels morally responsible for her death because, having concealed from her the fact of his "lawful" marriage, he is convinced that it was the discovery of his duplicity that killed the woman. He would then be trying to excuse himself here by saying that his wife had actually died before he met (married?) Mrs. Bathurst.

ness with the burden of his own thoughts, than "to throw life from him . . . for a little sleep."

It is in this desperate state of mind that Vickery, having fulfilled his commission at Bloemfontein, drops from sight, embarking on an aimless life as just another one of the many wandering tramps who people the back country. For Vickery is not unique in his inability to confront the world. "Takes 'em at all ages," says Pyecroft of another man who'd left his duty, and "We get heaps of tramps up there since the war," Hooper explains, suggesting that men trained in destruction or shaped by it must use their talents somehow, if only on themselves. Death is what Vickery is seeking, then, as he drifts from place to place, and he is not long in finding it. One day he and another tramp take refuge beside a railroad track during an electrical storm and there, beneath the teak trees, the two are struck by lightning and are burned to charcoal.[21] It is easily established that one of the two is Vickery, for Hooper happens coincidentally to be there, in his capacity as railroad inspector, to see the tattooed initials M.V. etched in white on the blackened corpse and to take from the crumbling jaws an undamaged dental plate identifiable as Vickery's. In fact, he has the plate in his waistcoat pocket but delicately refrains from showing it out of consideration for Pritchard's obvious distress. Vickery's death is bizarre, certainly, although it is based on a real incident with which Kipling was familiar. But what is really most striking about it is its appropriateness. The man who had been unable to cope with life's disorder achieves, at a stroke, by the accident of lightning, the final disorder of death. When Hooper tries to move the

---

21. Professor Robert Adams questions whether lightning could have had the effect described. There doesn't seem to be any very pleasant way of checking up on this, but perhaps we might graciously grant Kipling his carbonization as we grant Dickens and Charles Brockden Brown their spontaneous combustions.

scorched body from its position beside the track it literally crumbles to dust.

Critics have taken issue with the manner of Vickery's death, some suggesting that it is too accidental to be meaningful and aesthetically satisfying. An author, this argument runs, cannot express the idea of accidentalness by writing accidentally. Even an artist whose theme is chaos must portray it in terms of form. This criticism calls attention not only to Kipling's problem in this story but to the problem of all modern art. Samuel Beckett is recorded as having talked, a short while ago,

. . . about the tension in art between the mess and form. Until recently, [he said,] art has withstood the pressure of chaotic things. It realized that to admit them was to jeopardize form. 'How could the mess be admitted [when] it appears to be the very opposite of form and therefore destructive of the very thing that art holds itself to be?' But now we can keep it out no longer, because we have come into a time when 'it invades our experience at every moment. It is there and it must be allowed in.'[22]

In "Mrs. Bathurst," Kipling is dealing with what Beckett calls "the mess," and while we have a right to expect that he will give some kind of shape to his particular vision of life, we are wrong to require that shape to appear necessarily on the narrative level of the story. It is precisely on this level that we should expect, instead, to find all the craziness of life, all its meaninglessness. And a meaningless death may, after all, be thematically significant. Nor is it begging the question to say that "Mrs. Bathurst" has a form imposed upon it by its theme, the persistence of accident, the multiplications of what an existentialist might call the absurd. It is, in fact, just this reiteration of absurdity that is meant to satisfy our craving for form.

Vickery's story ends spectacularly, then, in the back country of South Africa, but some of the questions raised by that story still remain unanswered. Indeed we have still to consider what, for some reason, has always been the most controversial of all the "Mrs. Bathurst" problems, the identity of the second tramp. It was in *The Colophon* that J. Delancey Ferguson, in February, 1932, published an article which took for granted the fact that the tramp found beside Vickery in the teak forest was Mrs. Bathurst herself. Since that time this theory has gained great currency among readers who feel that the story would not be as good if Mrs. Bathurst were not the tramp, who feel that for a satisfying plot it is required that the two central figures be brought together at the close. Kipling was, however, constructing anything but a neat plot here; his central point was, of course, the untidiness of the universe. Mrs. Bathurst is not the conventional heroine of romantic fiction, hurrying to the side of her destitute lover and casting in her lot with his. In the light of the rest of the story this conception is difficult to accept. She is, rather, the unwitting agent of blind chance who dooms Vickery to death without even knowing she has done it. She is far away when the man dies and she knows nothing of what has happened to him, for the fates do not know or care what they have done and they do not die with their victims. It is in just these facts that the great sadness of the story lies, in just this failure of communication.[23]

---

23. There are other points to be made against the theory that the second tramp is Mrs. Bathurst. First, and quite conclusive by itself, is the fact that a railroad inspector friend of Hooper's had seen the two tramps shortly before the storm and had given them food and quinine. A man and a woman travelling together under those circumstances would surely have been conspicuous and would have made a first-rate story. The in-

Pritchard's last speech accents the blind impersonality of Mrs. Bathurst's power.

Pritchard covered his face with his hands for a moment, like a child shutting out an ugliness. 'And to think of her at Hauraki!' he murmured—with 'er 'air-ribbon on my beer. "Ada," she said to her niece . . . Oh, my Gawd!' . . . .

It has been suggested that this outburst could only be Pritchard's horrified reaction to the news that Mrs. Bathurst had been burnt to charcoal in the teak forest. But the speech has a different and perhaps greater significance. Throughout the narrative, Pritchard is presented to us as having himself fallen under Mrs. Bathurst's spell. He lovingly recounts his experience in the hotel bar at Hauraki

---

spector could hardly have resisted telling such a story to Hooper, had there been one, and Hooper would have had no reason to conceal the information from the other three men in the railroad car. But there was no story to tell. Later Hooper himself saw the pair and while identification might have been complicated by the condition of the bodies, it is plain that he took for granted that the two were men. "The man who was standin' up had the false teeth," he says casually, clearly implying that as far as he was concerned the squatting figure was also a man. It is difficult to think why Kipling would have put these details into his story had he intended the reader to think that the second tramp was Mrs. Bathurst.

But what, then, are we to make of the second tramp? Both J. M. S. Tompkins and C. A. Bodelsen have pointed out that it would have been unlike Kipling to introduce a wholly functionless character into one of his stories. Yet it is Miss Tompkins herself who suggests a function for the second tramp when she says (*The Art of Rudyard Kipling*, p. 90) that Vickery might have stood up deliberately in order to attract the lightning to himself—in order, like the groom in the epigraph, to "throw life from him for a little sleep." Assuming that Miss Tompkins was correct, how was Kipling to make such a point as this in a single tableau? Had Vickery been found alone, the fact that he was standing up could only with difficulty have been made to seem significant. The function of the second tramp, then, as he squats beside the tracks looking up, is to call our attention, by contrast, to Vickery's dangerous gesture.

For his part, Professor Bodelsen has concluded that the charred body of the second tramp is meant by Kipling to be the ghost of Mrs. Bathurst. *Aspects of Kipling's Art*, p. 145.

and at each suggestion that Mrs. Bathurst may have been even remotely responsible for what happened to Vickery, Pritchard protests vehemently—protests almost too much—that the lady could not have had anything to do with it. He seems to have a great stake in her innocence, and all through the story he rejects the truth which is dawning slowly on the others. But the horrible image of Vickery, totally consumed by his passion, finally breaks through his defenses and lets the truth pour in all at once. And the realization overwhelms him—he is, as we have seen, naturally emotional anyway—that Mrs. Bathurst, for all her innocence, has been profoundly involved in Vickery's fate. In his horror, Pritchard recalls what, up to that moment, had always been one of his pleasantest memories, the harmless flirtation in the Hauraki hotel. And understanding now the true nature of that blind, corrosive, impersonal attraction he had felt and himself almost succumbed to, he "covers his face with his hands for a moment, like a child shutting out an ugliness." Outside the office car, waiting for their train, the picnickers sing of romance in conventional, sentimental terms, offering an ironic contrast to Pritchard's belated revelation about the true nature of woman's love.

> On a summer afternoon, when the honeysuckle blooms,
>   And all Nature seems at rest,
> Underneath the bower, 'mid the perfume of the flower,
>   Sat a maiden with the one she loves the best.

It makes a properly bitter conclusion to a story which might equally well have ended with Kurtz's despairing words, "The horror, the horror!"

v

What happens in "Mrs. Bathurst" is, in the last analysis, a function of the work's structure.[24] All his life Kipling ex-

---

24. F. T. Cooper writes: "The whole strength of this story lies in the

perimented with techniques for drawing readers into the heart of a story, for forcing them, if possible, to participate in the creative process itself. In "Mrs. Bathurst," among other stories, he succeeded in a way which was to damage his popularity and earn him a reputation for trickiness. But it was in just such stories as this that he was most brilliantly the innovator, most startlingly the stylist ahead of his time. Of "Mrs. Bathurst" it can accurately be said that the structure is inextricably bound up with the content. "Mrs. Bathurst" is a story about a group of storytellers who are trying to put together a story and discover its meaning. The story they are constructing is also the one the reader must construct, so that the two activities go on simultaneously. The group of four men gathered in the railroad car to spin yarns is, like the cinema and the episode of Boy Niven, a metaphor for Kipling's vision of life: the irrationality of the universe and man's need to find some order in it. When the four come together, each of them, unknown to the others, has certain disordered fragments of a story, quite meaningless in themselves. (It would be more accurate to say that three of the members of the group have these fragments. The fourth member, the writer, will one day record the incidents.) They begin to chat idly, in a random way, and slowly, as they talk, a story begins to emerge a little haltingly from the anecdotes and the broken images that each contributes to the general store of information.

Even when all the fragments have been assembled it is plain that significant information is missing. But it is also plain that with just the pieces available to them they have

method of its telling. You hear it from the lips of stolid, callous naval men, rude of speech, coarse in their views of life in general and of women in particular. And through the medium of their very coarseness, their picturesque vulgarity, their lack of finer perceptions, you get an impression of a tragic drama which no amount of finer methods could have given." *Some English Story-Tellers*, p. 146.

made an important discovery which leaves them silent and disturbed. They have, in fact, discovered the theme of their own story, and though that discovery is never discussed in so many words, the same fragments of information which led the four narrators to their understanding are available to guide the reader to the same conclusions. Indeed, it is because what the storytellers do is so much the model for what Kipling would have his readers do that such emphasis is placed on the "picture-frame" elements in "Mrs. Bathurst." The process of telling the story is as important to an understanding of the whole as the incidents of the story themselves.

In order to tell his story in the way he wanted to, Kipling had to abandon certain of the conventions of prose fiction, most notably the convention of redundancy. The usual story writer, in an effort to achieve immediate clarity, gives his readers too much information. Composing a conversation between two engineers, for example, he will have one say to the other, "Do you think there's much chance of getting a bridge across the river at this point?" Kipling, in a similar situation, would be content with "Well, what do you think?"—a line which might leave the casual reader mystified but which would seem clear enough, in context, to one who had been following the story closely.

The trouble with conventional dialogue is, in the first place, that people do not really talk in exposition. They say just enough to make themselves understood by the people they are addressing and do not behave as if they were aware of a large, unseen audience requiring to be kept informed. More important, such dialogue stands between the reader and the narrative, rejecting the reader's cooperation by assuring him that he will learn all there is to learn about the story without any effort on his part. In Kipling's dialogue there are few independently meaningful lines; meaning emerges from the total organization of what has

gone before and what is to come. Description here is something more than decoration; it is a background against
which individually obscure lines take on significance. A
gesture will often finish a sentence. This kind of dialogue
stretches the mind, requires, in Miss Tompkins' words, "a
full participation of the imagination"[25] by readers who,
like Pyecroft, recognize that seeing and hearing are not
the only regulation aids to ascertaining facts.

There are many examples of this sort of dialogue in "Mrs.
Bathurst." One toward the end of the story is representative. Hooper, speaking of his journey up-country on railroad business, says

"I was up there a month ago relievin' a sick inspector, you
see. He told me to look out for a couple of tramps in the teak."
"Two?" Pyecroft said. "I don't envy that other man if—"

Pyecroft's aposiopesis, out of context, would be meaningless. It is probably meaningless, in any case, to casual readers of the story who have forgotten about Vickery's lunacy
and murderous threats and Pyecroft's fear of being alone
with the man. Those who have not forgotten are in a position to reconstruct the end of the sentence and so to participate, with the author and the four men in the railroad
car, in the creation of the story.

The whole narrative may, in fact, be considered an extended example of aposiopesis. Hooper brings his hand to
his waistcoat pocket, presumably to remove Vickery's
teeth, but the hand comes away empty. Pyecroft seems on
the verge of learning from Vickery's own lips the story of
his affair with Mrs. Bathurst, but Vickery breaks off, saying,
"The rest is silence." We are left to guess what exactly happened between Vickery and the captain, what Vickery did
as a tramp up-country, and who his companion was. The

25. Tompkins, p. 89.

tale of "Mrs. Bathurst," like Kipling's irrational universe, mocks our desire for reasonable explanations. Yet in the end, the theme of the story emerges clearly out of the calculated obscurity of the style.

Some aspects of that style are remarkable because of the way they foreshadow similar techniques in writers we are accustomed to thinking of as more serious. "Mrs. Bathurst" was published in 1904, some months before Leopold Bloom took his memorable walk through Dublin and many years before Joyce began to record the event. Yet this story uses a number of the narrative and structural devices which Joyce was to make famous in *Ulysses*. On the second page of "Mrs. Bathurst," for example, Hooper says

"That reminds me," he felt in his waistcoat pocket, "I've got a curiosity for you from Wankies—beyond Bulawayo. It's more of a souvenir perhaps than—"

Here he is interrupted by the precipitate entrance of Pyecroft and Pritchard, and it is not till the very end of the story that we learn the significance of those words and that casual gesture. In *Ulysses*, Bloom, putting on his hat in the morning "peeped quickly inside the leather headband. White slip of paper. Quite safe." The explanation of this slip of paper comes only several episodes later when we read "His right hand came down into the bowl of his hat. His fingers found quickly a card behind the headband and transferred it to his waistcoat pocket." Still later we find Bloom handing this card in at the post office. As Stuart Gilbert points out, "These fragments would seem meaningless to a reader who had forgotten the earlier passages; the broken phrases assume an order only when 'an hypothesis is thrown among them.' "[26]

---

26. Stuart Gilbert, *James Joyce's* Ulysses (New York, 1955), pp. 25-26.

In his study of *Ulysses*, Gilbert further shows how each of the episodes in Joyce's book has, among other things, an art, a symbol and a "technic" of its own. Remarkably enough, "Mrs. Bathurst" may be analyzed in just this way. Its "technic" is the movie newsreel whose structure serves as a model for the structure of the story just as a fugue and a labyrinth give structure to two of the episodes in *Ulysses*. The symbol in "Mrs. Bathurst" is the story-teller, representing man's eternal quest for the meaning concealed in random events. And the art of the story is aposiopesis, the device of classical rhetoric which seeks, on every level of the narrative, to withhold the ultimate secret.

It is not intended that this comparison with *Ulysses* should be anything but suggestive. What it suggests is the concentrated creative energy which Kipling brought to bear on "Mrs. Bathurst," the self-consciousness, in the good sense of that word, of his art. And if there is some question about the necessity for such self-consciousness, we need only try to imagine this story told in more conventional terms. What would be missing would be precisely that tension, precisely that feverish sense of strain which Kipling deliberately sought to achieve. The style may be tortured and convoluted, but it is not tricky. It is exactly the right style for conveying to the reader both the subject and the theme of "Mrs. Bathurst."

CHAPTER FIVE ▨

Imperialism as Metaphor

i

Having questioned the idea that Kipling was on the one hand too simple and on the other too trickily complex to be capable of serious art, I can now return to a consideration of some of the issues raised in my reading of "Without Benefit of Clergy." I suggested there that the aesthetic success of the story makes the matter of Kipling's attitude toward colonialism irrelevant in that context. But colonialism in the context of Kipling's work as a whole can hardly be considered irrelevant. Indeed, attacks on Kipling for his approval of the British presence in India, for his support of what Lionel Trilling has a called "a puny and mindless imperialism,"[1] have been, and continue to be, the most damaging of all criticisms leveled at the author. In part this has been true because, while the presumed trickiness and journalistic superficiality for which the writer has also been taken to task might actually recommend him in certain contemporary literary and art circles, and while the alleged violence in his work (of which I will speak later in detail) might even render him indistinguishable from a number of other modern fiction writers, his approval of imperialism, for just the reason that it implies acceptance of a number of stable social and cultural values, seems to

---

1. Lionel Trilling, "Kipling," *The Liberal Imagination* (New York, 1950), p. 126.

call into question the assault on those values which is the essence of contemporary art and violent fiction.

To put it another way, the rejection of imperialism in the twentieth century amounts to a rejection of the sort of rational materialism which, while it had already ceased, on the purely theoretical level, to have much vitality in the second half of the nineteenth century, nevertheless continued to underlie many of the political and social structures of the period. Thus, the average nineteenth-century man who believed in imperialism necessarily believed, first, in the physical and moral superiority of the colonialists; second, in the (at least temporary) physical and moral inferiority of the natives; and third, in the possibility that the colonialists, by their presence and through their efforts, might improve the lot of the natives. We think very differently about such matters today. The cultural relativism of the twentieth century, our age's loss of faith in the dogmas of science and progress, have swept away most of the philosophical foundations of imperialism; for us, therefore, it is impossible to treat the idea of an altruistic colonialism with anything but cynicism and contempt. It is not surprising, then, that Kipling's imperialism has been so damaging to his cause in the twentieth century, not surprising that so many readers have found the writer repugnant and have been repelled by such smugly self-satisfied passages as these:

There is a destiny now possible to us, the highest ever set before a nation to be accepted or refused. We are still undegenerate in race; a race mingled of the best northern blood . . . This is what England must either do, or perish; she must found colonies as fast and as far as she is able, formed of her most energetic and worthiest men; . . . their first aim is to advance the power of England by land and by sea.

> The noblest men methinks are bred
> Of ours the Saxon-Norman race. . . .

I

'Sweet, blighted lilies,'—as the American epitaph on the Nigger child has it,—sweet, blighted lilies, they are holding up their heads again! How pleasant in the universal bankruptcy abroad . . . to have always this fact to fall back upon: our beautiful Black darlings are at least happy; with little labour except to the teeth, *which* surely, in those excellent horse-jaws of theirs, will not fail.

[On the map] there was a vast amount of red—good to see at any time, because one knows that some real work is done in there.

If [such men] hadn't worked and died in England for thousands of years, you and I couldn't sit here without having our throats cut. There would be no trains, no ships to carry us literary people about in, no fields even. Just savagery. . . . More and more do I refuse to draw my income and sneer at those who guarantee it.

> Look left, look right, the hills are bright,
>   The dales are light between,
> Because 'tis fifty years tonight
>   That God has saved the Queen. . . .

> Oh, God will save her, fear you not:
>   Be you the men you've been,
> Get you the sons your fathers got,
>   And God will save the Queen.

I really think that the most living clue of life is in us Englishmen in England, and the great mistake we make is in not uniting together . . . and so carrying the vital spark through. Because as far as we are concerned it is in danger of being quenched. I know now it is a shirking of the issue to look to Buddha or the Hindu . . . for the impulse to carry through. . . . Those natives are *back* of us—in the living sense lower than we are. But they're going to swarm over us and suffocate us. We are, have been for five hundred years, the growing tip. Now we're going to fall. But you don't catch me going back on my whiteness and Englishness and myself.

The population should be homogeneous; where two or more cultures exist in the same place they are likely either to be fiercely self-conscious or both to become adulterate. What is still more important is unity of religious background; and reasons of race and religion combine to make any large number of free-thinking Jews undesirable. There must be a proper balance between urban and rural, industrial and agricultural development, and a spirit of excessive tolerance is to be deprecated.

What is, for our purposes, most interesting and instructive about these quotations is a fact about them which has no doubt already become quite evident to the reader: namely, that not one of them is by Rudyard Kipling. Instead, they are, respectively, the work of John Ruskin, Alfred, Lord Tennyson, Thomas Carlyle, Joseph Conrad, E. M. Forster, A. E. Housman, D. H. Lawrence, and T. S. Eliot. The significance of such a poor sleight-of-hand trick as this should not be misconstrued. This collection of chauvinistic and racist statements by famous authors is not intended to excuse similar comments by Kipling, of which there have been many, though none so virulent as the passages by Carlyle and Eliot. It is, however, intended to set Kipling's own statements in their proper context for the purpose of making a curious observation about the writer and his reputation.

The context is immediately established by the range of these quotations. Covering as they do a period from the middle of the nineteenth century through the first third of the twentieth, they represent many decades of uncritical acceptance, by some of the most revered writers of English literature, of what today seem outrageously bigoted or jingoistic ideas. Nor is this collection of excerpts in any sense exhaustive. Quotations from Yeats or Shaw or Pound, for example, might easily have replaced any of those included here without the list becoming any less out-

rageous in the process. These facts have never been a
secret, and most recently they have been examined by
John R. Harrison in *The Reactionaries: Yeats, Lewis,
Pound, Eliot, Lawrence*, a full-length study of what the
author calls "the anti-democratic intelligentsia."

It is precisely because Kipling can be read in the context
of such writers that it is possible to make the curious observation about him to which I have already referred, an
observation which can perhaps best be explained through
consideration of the final quotation on our list, the one by
T. S. Eliot. That passage is for us the most useful of the
excerpts, among other reasons because its urbane cruelty
makes it more repellent even than Carlyle's hysteria, and
because the date of its composition—1932—renders it particularly unforgivable, unforgivable in a way that the Ruskin and Tennyson statements, for example—written out of
a kind of political naiveté—are not. (By way of contrast,
Kipling in 1932 was vainly calling the attention of his
countrymen to the rise of totalitarianism in Germany and
was preparing to renounce the swastika as his personal
good luck sign because he felt Hitler was defiling it.)

Now what is most interesting about the Eliot statement
is that, though it is a reasonably well-known passage, and
though it expresses ideas which most critics vigorously op-
pose, its existence has never seriously interfered with the
admiration which many of these same critics have long felt
for T. S. Eliot's art. That is, the poems and plays go on being read and discussed and praised just as if their author
had not revealed himself, in political utterances such as
these, to be a man of arrogance and insensitivity. To be
sure, some critics, notably of the *Scrutiny* group,[2] have attacked the poet on political and moral grounds, have seen,

2. See, for example, Boris Ford's "A Case for Kipling?" *The Importance of Scrutiny* (New York, 1948).

in the conservatism, the traditionalism, the orthodox mysticism of the poems, counterparts of the ideas embodied in the quotation. In the main, however, it would be safe to say that for most readers of T. S. Eliot, political passages such as the one we have presented here are largely irrelevant to an appreciation and an evaluation of the poet's art.

The same may be said of all of these quotations. Critics have long been aware of their existence, have not hesitated to refer to them scathingly wherever such reference has seemed appropriate to a discussion of their authors, but have not, for the most part, allowed what are essentially political comments to distract literary criticism from its real business, the judgment of art. Only with Kipling—and here we come to the curious observation of which I have spoken—have the critics abandoned their sound policy of clearly differentiating between an artist's works and his personal opinions. As a result, of all the writers belonging to the "anti-democratic intelligentsia" during the late nineteenth century and after, Kipling is the only one whose works continue today to be dismissed as unworthy of serious critical consideration largely because their author's social theories are offensive; the only one, that is, whose politics are still examined with greater care than his poems and stories.

One explanation for this phenomenon may lie in the fact that Kipling is of historical interest in a way that most other writers of English literature are not. That is, his association with India and with the Anglo-Indian experience is different in kind from the association of, say, Dickens with London or of Jane Austen with Bath. For Kipling was the only writer of quality produced by the British community in India who devoted himself to extensive recording of the life of that community in his art, and so for better or worse his pictures are the only really vital ones available of many facets of the English colonial experiment: his soldiers the only ones who have survived the marches and barracks of a hundred years ago, his civil servants the only members of that strange breed who live today outside the pages of the old departmental reports. Thus for students of the period Kipling is, unavoidably, the raw data for history books, a fact which discourages purely aesthetic consideration of his work.

More to the point, however, in explaining the political bias of much Kipling criticism is the matter of what I have called the artist's "voice." When we listen, for example, to the sound of the T. S. Eliot passage, what we hear is a remote, disinterested, aristocratic voice, the voice of a visionary amateur making metaphors, and our impulse, like that of the *Scrutiny* critic, is to recognize in that voice the note of idealistic ardor which is also to be heard in the poems, but to dismiss the passage out of hand as serious political theorizing. Thus, we are able to judge the quotation to be very seriously in error without allowing a purely political pronouncement to affect our opinion of Eliot as an artist. When Kipling, on the other hand, speaks of political matters, he does so, if not in a "lower-middle-class snarl of defeated gentility,"[3] then certainly in the voice of the man-who-has-had-to-meet-a-payroll, the knowledgeable common soldier, the worker on the job. He deliberately adopts, that is, the tone of someone who knows what he is talking about from hard, practical experience, and it is perhaps a tribute to the success with which he is able to project this voice-of-the-insider that when we judge Kipling's ideas to be wrong, we consider his failure to be much more serious than Eliot's. He is not, after all, merely a poet waxing mystical about matters outside his field of special competence. He is very specifically talking—so his tone of voice seems to be telling us—of matters within his field of

---

3. Trilling, p. 125.

special competence. Therefore when he is wrong, our impulse is to hold him strictly accountable for his errors.

It must be emphasized again, however, that the voice of the expert we hear in Rudyard Kipling's stories and poems is every bit as much an artifact[4] as the voice that speaks in T. S. Eliot's poems and plays. Where such a story, poem or play fails as a work of art—where, that is, its voice seems to be imposed upon it from outside rather than proceeding organically from within—we may imagine that the author has deliberately set out to convince us of his ideas in his own person and that it is to those ideas that we are being asked to attend. We must remember, however, that the significant failure in such cases is always the aesthetic rather than the political one; that the issue is always the inability of the work of art to justify its ideas rather than the failure of the ideas to justify themselves. In the matter of Kipling's colonialism, therefore, the question is not whether the imperial idea *per se* is or is not a good one; instead, the issue is whether or not, in a given story or poem, the idea of colonialism has a valid artistic function to perform.

For Kipling the artist, colonialism is (as the Jew is for Eliot) always more important as a metaphor than as an abstract or even than as a practical idea. One critic has recently written that for Kipling the British Empire

was really a macrocosm, or a huge wall against which the shadows of private emotions, personal actions, might be enormous-

---

4. To take one example, the construction scenes in the first half of "The Bridge-Builders" may not, for all their specificity, be as accurate as they seem. A civil engineer assured Walter M. Hart, on one occasion, that Kipling's bridge-building was nonsense (See *Kipling the Story-Writer*, p. 169), and alert readers have uncovered similar mistakes in other of the author's technical descriptions. This suggests that it was an old habit with Kipling to adopt, for aesthetic reasons, the voice of the expert in situations where he had no expertise, and it warns us not to take what that voice has to say too literally.

ly thrown. The conflicts [he] portrayed were not essentially political conflicts, however dressed up in heroics and empire-building, but were just those stresses between man and his environment, spaciously and sometimes violently expressed, which lay near the roots of all romantic art.[5]

Numbers of Kipling's works attest to this fact. One story, for example, in which imperialism is "a huge wall against which the shadows of private emotions, personal actions, are enormously thrown" is "The Bridge-Builders," a long, complex tale, collected in a volume Kipling called *The Day's Work*. The title of the book is significant, a reference to the quotation from Carlyle's *Sartor Resartus* (and ultimately from John 9.4) which Lockwood Kipling carved over his son's fireplace in Brattleboro, Vermont: "Work while it is called today, for the night cometh wherein no man can work." It is by now a truism that work was for Kipling, as it was for Carlyle, an almost mystical act, the one means—both authors agreed—by which a human being is capable of discovering and realizing himself in the world, of making his spirit flesh, so to speak. Kipling came to this position through many early and painful experiences with protracted hard work. "I discovered that a man can work with a temperature of 104," he recalls about himself at seventeen, newly arrived in a sweltering Indian newspaper office, "even though next day he has to ask the office who wrote the article."[6] And further along in his memoir he speaks eloquently of working with

the taste of fever in one's mouth, and the buzz of quinine in one's ears; the temper frayed by heat to the breaking-point, but for sanity's sake held back from the break . . .[7]

---

5. From an unsigned review, in *TLS* (6 July 1967), 596, of Alan Sandison's *The Wheel of Empire: A Study of the Imperial Idea in some late Nineteenth- and Early Twentieth-Century Literature* (London, 1967).

6. Rudyard Kipling, *Something of Myself* (New York, 1937), p. 47.

7. *Something of Myself*, p. 68.

It was through experiences such as these during what he called, in *Something of Myself*, "seven years hard" that Kipling developed a mystique of work naturally associated in his mind with colonialism, the particular social structure within which his labors were performed. And it is for this reason that over the years, and just as naturally, colonialism became for him less an abstract political theory than an almost private metaphor for self-discovery and self-fulfilment. If we wish, then, to come to terms with imperialism in Kipling's art, we should try to see it as the author saw it in a story like "The Bridge-Builders"; see it, that is, as an aesthetic as well as a political expression, as a metaphor for "the day's work," with all the overtones of the spirit-made-flesh which a quasi-religious view of the day's .work implies.

ii

"The Bridge-Builders" is, like Kipling's later story "The Gardener," a tale which opens in a perfectly straight-forward, realistic way, only to become complicated, as the narrative develops, by elements of the supernatural. The world we encounter at the beginning of the story is delineated with photographic realism. Indeed, the early passages seem to have been specifically designed to create a sense of life-as-it-really-is, for they are full of particulars about the tough, no-nonsense business of building a bridge. On the very first page, for example, we are given an engineer's view of the span and its environs, a description crowded with what appear to be quite enough details to permit a clever reader to reproduce the whole structure himself. "With the bridge's approaches," we read, Findlayson's work

was one mile and three-quarters in length; a lattice-girder bridge, trussed with the Findlayson truss, standing on seven-

and-twenty brick piers. Each one of those piers was twenty-four feet in diameter, capped with red Agra stone and sunk eighty feet below the shifting sand of the Ganges' bed. Above them ran the railway-line fifteen feet broad; above that, again, a cart-road of eighteen feet, flanked with footpaths. . . .

The atmosphere of the second half of the story could not be more different from that of the first. Where, in the early pages of the tale, the author's material consists largely of Englishmen and English ways, efficient engineering and, in general, the practical affairs of the world, in the later sections the subject matter changes to include, instead, lethargic, tradition-ridden India and the opium-dulled world of the supernatural. The setting changes too, in keeping with the change of subject matter, and from the scarred, cluttered site of the great bridge, "ugly as original sin," we are swept by the Ganges down to a small island crowded with mysterious presences out of India's past. In short, the contrast between the two halves of the tale—between the real world and the "fabulous" world of dreams,[8] out of which is to emerge the theme of the story—is clear and crucial; indeed, it is hinted at as early as the narrative's opening lines. "The least that Findlayson, of the Public Works Department, expected was a C. I. E.," Kipling tells us, and then goes on, joining the issue at once, "he dreamed of a C. S. I."

From the technical point of view, what is perhaps most remarkable about these contrasting worlds of "The Bridge-Builders" is the fact that Kipling was able to incorporate them both into a single tale without destroying the unity of his work. In "The Gardener," another story dealing with different levels of existence, the supernatural experience is

8. Significantly, Bonamy Dobrée has subtitled his most recent study of Kipling "Realist and Fabulist," thus emphasizing two sides of the author's vision which are especially developed in "The Bridge-Builders."

a momentary one, and its introduction into the narrative is quite consciously designed to be shocking. The theme of "The Gardener," we have seen, specifically calls for this treatment of the material. Only a profound shock can be of any use to Helen Turrell, steeped as she is in self-deception and defeat, and the story is deliberately constructed to supply that shock.

"The Bridge-Builders," however, has something very different to say and so has a very different structure. It contains no shock at all. Instead, the real world blends so imperceptibly into the world of the supernatural—steam engines and talking elephants exist so comfortably side by side—that for all the violent contrasts inherent in the subject matter of the story, the reader often has the sense of viewing not two worlds but one. This, of course, is precisely Kipling's point; that the India of which he writes—the India of this very special instant of history—stands between two ways of life in a world all its own, a world in which, without the slightest self-consciousness, a man may at one moment pray to a river, the next to the dome of a cathedral, and the next to a low-press cylinder in an engine room; a world in which an anachronistic hereditary ruler can steam up a river in a boat whose mechanism he has not yet learned to understand, to participate in a religious ceremony in which he no longer believes.

The delicate shading of the world of reality into the world of dreams, through which Kipling makes this point in "The Bridge-Builders," is another illustration of the author's technical skill. The vehicle for the transition is the consciousness of Chief Engineer Findlayson as it gradually alters under the influence of opium. Kipling is careful, however, not to describe this alteration directly. Wanting the change to be imperceptible, he tries to divert our attention from the moment when it is actually occurring by continuing to describe events, as he has been doing quite matter-of-factly all along, through the Chief Engineer's eyes. Thus, it is only by noticing changes in Findlayson's perceptions of distance and time that we can begin to infer the effects of the drug on the man's mind.[9]

Such indirection has a purpose. Kipling could have described Findlayson's encounter with the raging river in straightforward, realistic terms. He might easily have pictured in detail the sinking of the boat, the wallowing of the men in the river, the striking out for land and the discovery of the deserted island. Instead, as we have seen, he chose to portray not the events themselves but rather Findlayson's distorted reactions to those events, for his object was to communicate something more than simple melodrama. By picturing, for example, the separation of the engineer's soul and body and their painful reunion a moment later, Kipling was writing a scene which served

---

9.   Kipling liked to use this indirect method of describing events, even when its employment was not so clearly justified as it is in "The Bridge-Builders." In the last scene of "The Brushwood Boy," for example, as Georgie and Miriam come slowly to understand the truth about the dreams they have been mysteriously sharing all their lives, the moment inevitably arrives for the lovers' first kiss. For some reason, however, Kipling cannot bring himself to describe the scene directly, preferring, instead, to concentrate on how the action affects some rather unlikely witnesses. "What does it mean?" Miriam asks, alluding to the remarkable fate that has befallen them.

"This," said Georgie. The horses quickened their pace. They thought they had heard an order.

It is a clever touch, but in this case it only compounds the coyness of the entire scene and might well have been omitted.

Using the same technique in *Something of Myself* (p. 248), Kipling writes:

My treatment of books, which I looked upon as tools of my trade, was popularly regarded as barbarian. Yet I economized on my multitudinous penknives, and it did no harm to my forefinger.

J. M. S. Tompkins refers to the device as the technique of submerged narrative, one of the most extended examples of which, as we have seen, is "Mrs. Bathurst."

two purposes. He was presenting, by inference, the details of the action in the river—in this case the shock of water in the engineer's lungs restoring him, for an instant, to himself. But in addition, he was conveying, with his image of the released soul, a sense of mystical detachment; was preparing the way, as it were, for the talking beast-Gods of the island and all their magical trappings. In short, what he was subtly accomplishing, with his technique of indirection, was to bridge the gap between the world of reality in the first half of his story and the world of the supernatural in the second.

That Kipling should have constructed so elaborate a bridge passage is, of course, no accident. The story is, after all, one about bridge-builders, and our attention is called very particularly to the metaphoric nature of the title by the monkey god Hanuman. "Ho! Ho!" he says, "I am the builder of bridges indeed—bridges between this and that, and each bridge leads surely to Us in the end." It is natural, then, to find the author building a bridge of his own in this tale, eager as he always was that his theme should emerge not simply from the narrative details of his story but from the structural elements as well. In "The Bridge-Builders," the theme emerges in just this way. The huge bridge over the Ganges linking the two shores, Findlayson's narcotic descent of the river linking the daylight world of reality with the nighttime world of dreams—these join with the structure of the story to emphasize Kipling's point: that the particular work of these particular Englishmen in India is to provide a bridge from an old world of dying gods to a new and a freer life.

Stated baldly in this way, such a theme is open to a good deal of misinterpretation, for what the author seems to be saying is that the British are somehow naturally superior to the Indians and that their way of life is therefore automatically better. Many Kipling critics, some of them quite friendly ones, have represented the author's views in these terms, Rupert Croft-Cooke, for example, speaking of Kipling's hero-worship of "such men as Findlayson," and commenting that the author's experiences in the East had taught him respect for "government of the naturally governable by the natural ruler."[10]

Whether or not Kipling ever took such an extreme position in his personal life, it is clear he took no such position in "The Bridge-Builders," the story to which Croft-Cooke particularly alludes. The text itself indicates this. In it the author goes out of his way to show that Findlayson's stature is the result of personal courage and clear-sightedness and is not an automatic function of the fact that he is white and English. There are many other white men working on the bridge-building project,

labour-contractors by the half-hundred—fitters and riveters, European, borrowed from the railway workshops, with perhaps twenty white and half-caste subordinates to direct, under direction, the bevies of workmen,

but there are none in whom Findlayson and Hitchcock can place absolute trust. As for any special competence residing in the English, Kipling easily explodes that notion. It is the British Government in India which nearly wrecks the bridge with its uninformed meddling, and it is Englishmen at home whom Hitchcock must overcome before work can proceed. Thus, being white or being British is no guarantee of greatness in "The Bridge-Builders." Indeed, the one other man on the project whom Findlayson and his lieutenant can rely on almost as much as they can rely on themselves is a native.

Other readers have seen other things in "The Bridge-

---

10.   Rupert Croft-Cooke, *Rudyard Kipling* (London, 1958), p. 25.

Builders": an expression of Kipling's faith, for example, that bridges and locomotives could be substituted for India's centuries-old culture as an answer to all of the country's problems. The idea gains a certain support from anecdotes which have always circulated about Kipling's popular Victorian faith in the efficacy of machinery. In one sense, the author brought this reputation on himself with his many tales about steamships, locomotives and automobiles, but the fact of the matter is that Kipling's notions of progress were never so naive as these stories made them appear. As early as 1891, for example, he was recording, with ill-concealed contempt, conversations he had heard during a trip to Chicago.

I listened to people who said that the mere fact of spiking down strips of iron to wood, and getting a steam and iron thing to run along them was progress, that the telephone was progress, and the network of wires overhead was progress.[11]

"The Bridge-Builders" itself refutes the notion that Kipling thought mechanical ingenuity for its own sake was any sort of step forward. It quite accurately points out, for example, how the very efficiency of the new railway system hastens the spread of disease. "[I have] bound the sickness to the wheels of the fire-carriages," says the tigress Kali, Mother of Death, "so that it [runs] from one end of the land to the other."

There have been still other readings of the story. J. M. S. Tompkins has suggested, for example, that "The Bridge-Builders" is a celebration of the healing power of work, that Findlayson, back from his experience on the enchanted island and shaken by his insight into the abyss, turns gratefully to his work again to drive out the truths he has learned. Up to a point, Miss Tompkins is correct.

---

11. Rudyard Kipling, *American Notes* (Boston, 1899), p. 98.

To the extent that she finds Kipling using work as a metaphor for creativity, for the way in which man is most like
God, she is right to speak of its healing powers. When,
however, she sees Findlayson—so proud of his ability to
confront the world as it really is without flinching or looking away—as a man who buries himself in his work in order
to avoid the truth about life, she is less convincing. Findlayson returns, she writes, "shutting his mind easily to his
vision. . . . It is necessary to man's health in this world that
he should be shortsighted." He must not watch "the great
tides of the universe."[12] In fact, however, Kipling does not
present Findlayson as a man for whom work is a means of
avoiding reality. Indeed, the conscious creative drive of
Findlayson's work brings him face to face with every
agency of chaos imaginable, from bureaucratic interfer-
ence to natural disaster. It may be, Kipling sees, that for
some men work is a drug, but for the most conscious men
it is not often a very efficacious drug. In "Without Benefit
of Clergy," for example, Holden's office duties do not relieve him of anxiety and pain, and in "The Bridge-Builders" Kipling specifically represents such purposeless work-
for-its-own-sake as one of life's old illusions, an act of self-
deception coming under the direct control of one of the
old Gods. "The fire-carriages bring me new worshippers
from beyond the Black Water," says the monkey-God,
"the men who believe that their God is toil. I run before
them beckoning, and they follow Hanuman."

iii

What, then, is "The Bridge-Builders" all about? What is
the nature of the new, freer life which Kipling suggests is

---

12. J. M. S. Tompkins, *The Art of Rudyard Kipling* (London, 1959), p. 193.

just across the river, opening out, so to speak, at the far end of Findlayson's bridge? And what has the bridge to do with that life? These are the central questions of the story. They are also the questions which trouble the beast-Gods who have convened, at the request of one of their number, on an island in the middle of the Ganges. The parley of the animals begins as Mother Gunga (the Ganges), in the shape of a huge crocodile or "mugger," emerges from her already receding waters to bewail her ignominious captivity. "They have made it too strong for me," she complains about the great bridge that is now her yoke. "In all this night I have only torn away a handful of planks. The walls stand! The towers stand! They have chained my flood, and my river is not free anymore."

Such anger and despair are obviously genuine, but the other animal-Gods do not respond with much sympathy to the mugger's call for justice. Indeed, they accept the bridge and its affront to the river with a curious equanimity, each, in his own way, minimizing the seriousness of this latest challenge to the power of the Gods. For over the centuries they have met and overcome many such challenges, and this new attack seems to them no different from all the others. Hanuman, as we have noted, sees the bridge, the fire-carriages and all the other mechanical contrivances which the British have introduced into India as just so many more ritualistic offerings of "the men who believe that their God is toil." Bridge-builders are, by a simple process of transference, worshippers of Hanuman, the god of work, and Hanuman is satisfied. Ganesh the elephant, God of the "fat money-lenders," is also satisfied. For looking at the account books over the shoulders of his clerks, he sees the foreign names, the records of many transactions, the accumulation of wealth, and knowing that such plenty is the result of the fire-carriages and of the bridges

K

over which they pass, he cannot, in his heart, be angry at
the yoke which Mother Gunga finds so galling.

The other Gods are also unperturbed by the river's distress. Bhairon, the drunken God of the Common Man, sees
that the fire-carriages bring thousands of pilgrims to this
shrine, and he is content, while Kali, the tigress Mother of
Death, is happy that these same machines have become
speedy, efficient carriers of disease. Not even the new religion which accompanies the railroads and the bridges
disturbs the old, established Gods. They have seen and assimilated many such religions. "Their gods!" Mother
Gunga says with contempt. "What should their Gods
know? They were born yesterday, and those that made
them are scarcely yet cold." And Hanuman, reporting that
already in the South the new woman God called Mary is
pictured with twelve arms, is told by Kali, "I am that
Woman."

To the Gods on the island, then, the bridge over the
Ganges does not appear to be a threat, does not seem to
portend any drastically new way of life. Yet Mother
Gunga's complaints persist, and she is soon joined in her
foreboding by the God Krishna. Krishna, the Well-Be-
loved, protector of earthly love, has arrived rather belated-
ly at the island meeting, but he is able to confirm Mother
Gunga in her intimations of disaster for the Gods, intimations which become quite explicit at this point in the narrative and which—the reader may now begin to see—have
all along been carefully prepared for by a special aspect
of the story's structure. For from the first, Kipling has been
cleverly playing upon conventional expectations in this
tale in his effort to establish that the bridge which so in-
furiates Mother Gunga is in fact a very real threat to all
the Gods.

His device is a simple one, based on the literary commonplace that in serious stories which pit a man-made work against the uncontrolled fury of nature, nature always wins. This is not so much a cliché as it is a classic metaphor for man's presumption and for the inevitability of his fall, and from the first "The Bridge-Builders" seems to be following this classic pattern. There is the great bridge, almost—but not quite—finished; there is the impressive engineer, betting everything on the invulnerability of his equations; there are the vaguely troubling rumors of approaching catastrophe ("What think you Mother Gunga will say when the rail runs over?"); and finally, there is the terrible, admonishing rage of Nature. It is no wonder that when Findlayson, in his delirium, speaks of the deluge having already swept his work away, we are quite prepared to write off the audacity of the great bridge as just another instance of hubris. How much more startling it is, then, against a background of such expectations as these, to hear Mother Gunga announce, "They have made it too strong for me." Immediately, we become aware that this is not to be the story we had expected and that Findlayson's bridge is not to be the usual symbol of man's vanity after all. Instead we find that there has been subtly implanted in our minds the idea of the bridge as a new and potent force in the world; precisely the idea which Krishna, on behalf of the grumbling Mother Gunga, tries to convey to the other Gods on the island.

At first the others remain wholly unmoved by Krishna's warning, despite its eloquence. "A new word," the young protector of love and life says, "is creeping from mouth to mouth among the Common Folk . . . saying (and none know who set that word afoot) that they weary of ye, Heavenly Ones." But the Gods only laugh together softly at this prophesy, and Hanuman is quick to offer the time-honored response.

They will only change a little the names of their Gods. I shall lead the builders of the bridges as of old: Shiv shall be worshipped in the schools . . . Ganesh shall have his Mahajuns, and Bhairon the donkey-drivers, the pilgrims and the sellers of toys. Beloved, they will do no more than change the names, and that we have seen a thousand times.

But Krishna is not to be put off so easily and his response, based as it is upon his close acquaintance with men, chills even the most sanguine of the Gods.

They will change more than the names . . . Great Kings, the beginning of the end is born already. The fire-carriages shout the names of new Gods that are *not* the old under new names. . . . As men count time the end is far off; but as we who know reckon, it is today. I have spoken.

These last words are followed by a long, brooding silence. At last Indra, Father of all, is called upon to judge Krishna's warning, and the huge Buck answers obliquely with an allusion to the Riddle of the Gods. "When Brahm ceases to dream," he says, "the heavens and the hells and the earth disappear. Be content. Brahm dreams still. . . . Go, my children! Brahm dreams—and till He wakes the Gods die not." With this, day breaks, the waters of the Ganges recede, and the animal-Gods move off heavily, chastened by what they have heard from Krishna though still uncertain about the specific nature of this new power which is going to usurp their own.

Ironically, the person best able to explain the nature of that power—the architect of the bridge which is its symbol —is on the same island with the Gods. Glazed with opium and barely able to move, Findlayson is in no condition to offer such an explanation, but the changes which have taken place in his mind as a result of the drug are sufficiently revealing. From them we can infer the qualities which, under normal circumstances, contribute to the

Chief Engineer's strength, and it is that strength, Krishna
has told us, which is the real challenge to the authority of
the Gods.

The description of what opium does to Findlayson is
graphic. No sooner has the man swallowed the pellets
which Peroo has given him[13] than his view of the world
begins subtly to alter. Where, moments before, he had
been calculating with great precision the exact stresses and
strains on his bridge—the specific mathematical relationship between water and stone—he now begins to lose all
sense of the reality of that relationship. Thus, when Peroo
shouts that the stone boats are breaking free, Findlayson
conceives at once an immensely complex plan for recovering them, a plan which bears no relationship at all to the
real nature of the problem, but which instead is a crazy
hallucination, parodying the normally rational workings
of his mind.

He saw the ropes running from boat to boat in straight lines
and angles—each rope a line of white fire. But there was one
rope which was the master rope. He could see that rope. If he
could pull it once, it was absolutely and mathematically certain that the disordered fleet would reassemble itself.

The plan, of course, fails, and Findlayson, collapsing into
one of the boats, is whirled off down the river. In an instant
he has worked out still another scheme—one, this time,
which involves walking on water—and not many moments
later his total divorce from reality is symbolized by the
separation of his soul from his body.

The drugged Findlayson on the island is very different

---

13. Kipling says that Findlayson took the pills "hardly knowing what
he did." It is of interest that Holden's plunge into native ritual in "Without Benefit of Clergy" is prefaced by just these words, as if unconsciousness were the necessary prerequisite to such action.

from the man we meet at the beginning of the story, a man whose chief characteristic is a profound personal commitment to material reality. This Findlayson knows that there are laws governing the physical world, irrevocable structures in all things, and he accepts as self-evident that man's highest function is to confront the reality of these laws and structures and to bring the physical world gradually under control by the process of learning its principles and of struggling to apply them.

From the struggle there may occasionally arise such a victory as the bridge over the Ganges, a symbol of the subduing of nature and itself the product of a thousand encounters with an intransigent world. Nothing, the story points out, is easy in that world. Nothing ever falls into place of its own accord. Every victory, Findlayson knows,. must be fought for and must be deserved, and every victory involves the confronting and overcoming of some fact: the fact of indifference at home, the fact of bureaucracy, the fact of the tensile strength of steel and of the holding power of stone, the fact of cholera and the fact of time. Looking back over the construction of the bridge, Findlayson remembers how months of office work had once been destroyed at a blow "when the Government of India, at the last moment, added two feet to the width of the bridge, under the impression that bridges were cut out of paper." Such cavalier treatment of reality, Kipling means us to see, is the ultimate in blind destructiveness, and only serves to emphasize how valid and fruitful is Findlayson's own respect for the physical universe.

That respect is not the product of a shallow materialism,[14] though it is true that Findlayson's bridge is first of

---

14. Though it is remarkable how many critics have assumed, on the basis of traditional notions about Kipling and his work, that the author's vision of the material, and more specifically of the mechanical, world

all a piece of mechanical reality, a feat of engineering, and one which is successful only because hundreds of men have been willing to dedicate themselves to the drudgery of moving tons of rock and earth. But the bridge is more than the sum of its physical parts. It is also, as bridges have always been, a metaphor, a flight of imagination conquering time and space as well as stone and steel. Linking two shores, the structure links—in what is really a primal act of creativity—two worlds as well, so that the building of the bridge becomes, in the story, a metaphor for the central creative act of life, and Findlayson's vision of the universe emerges as a far-reaching philosophy rather than a narrow pragmatism.

That philosophy, like Ameera's in "Without Benefit of Clergy," is one of total dedication to the reality of experience, and in keeping with it Findlayson both literally and

---

must be superficial. John Bayley, for example, in *The Romantic Survival,* isolates Kipling's famous line about Romance bringing up the 9:15, and sees in it an essentially "light-weight" literary use of modern mechanical reality. The serious use of such reality, Bayley tells us, was envisaged by Wordsworth, who looked forward to a time when "what is now called science shall be ready to put on, as it were, a form of flesh and blood," and who thought that "the poet will lend his divine spirit to aid the transfiguration." Bayley sees Hart Crane's use of the Brooklyn Bridge as a praiseworthy, if unsuccessful, attempt to fulfill Wordsworth's prophesy, but he then goes on to make the questionable statement that

Crane does not fall into the error, as Kipling might well have done had he set out to romanticize the world of the machine on the same ambitious scale, of describing the industrial world for its own sake; he attempts to show how the creative imagination of man controls and harmonises with it. . . . (p. 7)

The passage implies, in the first place, that Kipling never did make an ambitious attempt to romanticize (in Bayley's rather specialized sense of the word) the world of the machine. But "The Bridge-Builders," one of the author's longest and most complex stories, must surely stand as such an attempt. Moreover, it is an attempt in which, clearly, Kipling is not satisfied to "describe the industrial world for its own sake," but one in which he very specifically tries to give to the mechanical reality of Findlayson's bridge the "form of flesh and blood," the incarnation which Wordsworth spoke of so eloquently.

figuratively gives himself to his work. On the first page of "The Bridge-Builders," we learn that

for three years he had endured heat and cold, disappointment, discomfort, danger, and disease, with responsibilities almost too heavy for one pair of shoulders; and day by day, through that time, the great Kashi Bridge over the Ganges had grown under his charge.

Indeed, the bridge, many parts of which bear Findlayson's own name, seems an incarnation of the architect—his spirit made substance—and the story misses no opportunity to emphasize this metaphor. When, for example, the flooding Ganges threatens Findlayson's bridge, the Chief Engineer finds himself recalling other men's disasters, and, considering the inevitable identification of the builders with their creations, he remembers "when Lockhart's big water-works burst and broke down in brick heaps and sludge, and Lockhart's spirit broke in him and he died." And he thinks of his own bridge

carrying the Findlayson truss as well as the new pier-shoe, the Findlayson bolted shoe. There were no excuses in his service. Government might listen, perhaps, but his own kind would judge him by his bridge, as that stood or fell.

The builder and his work, then, are identical. The creative impulse is one with its expression in stone and metal—indeed, has no real existence apart from that expression—and commitment to reality becomes the only possible way of life. It is for this reason that Krishna is represented as the one God who will survive the coming drastic change in the world order. For Krishna is the only God who walks among men, who has committed himself to flesh, who has accepted the reality and the significance of human experience; the one God for whom, in Robert Frost's words, merit lies "in risking spirit/In substantiation."[15] Findlayson also derives his creative power from an absolute acceptance of physical reality. Like any artist, he pays the material universe the compliment of taking it seriously, and in a personal act of substantiation—in building the bridge—he renders to it all of his energy. It is an act symbolized in the story by the coming together again of the engineer's momentarily dissociated body and soul. Of that trauma of incarnation Kipling writes, "The pain of the reunion was atrocious, but it was necessary, also, to fight for the body."

Seen in terms such as these, Findlayson, the bridge-builder, is indeed a threat to the old Gods of India, for his almost mystical faith in the validity of "real" experience endangers their very existence. One passage in particular makes this clear. Day is dawning on the island in the Ganges, the animal Gods have broken up their council, and Findlayson is just shaking off the effects of Peroo's opium pellets, the last words of the God Indra still lingering in his mind: "Brahm dreams—and till He wakes the Gods die not." Peroo, chattering about the strange experiences of the previous night, has occasion to ask "Has the Sahib forgotten; or do we black men only see the Gods?"

---

15. Robert Frost, *In the Clearing* (New York, 1957), epigraph. The whole passage reads:

> But God's own descent
> Into flesh was meant
> As a demonstration
> That the supreme merit
> Lay in risking spirit
> In substantiation.

Kipling turned to this idea again in "Dymchurch Flit," one of the stories in *Puck of Pook's Hill*. It is a tale about the driving of the "little people" out of England, and of all the supernatural creatures who once held sway over men's imaginations, only Puck or Robin Goodfellow is shown able to resist the pressure to leave; this because, as Kipling tells us, "he's cleaved middlin' close to people, like."

Findlayson replies, his mind already eager to return to reality, "It seemed that the island was full of beasts and men talking, but I do not remember. A boat could live in this water now, I think." And Peroo, suddenly understanding the significance of what he has heard, says "Oho! Then it *is* true. 'When Brahm ceases to dream, the Gods die.' Now I know, indeed, what he meant."

Peroo's discovery is easily interpreted. The native foreman has stumbled upon the answer to the Riddle of the Gods and has come to see that in terms of that riddle, Findlayson and Brahm are one and the same. Indeed, throughout the story the Chief Engineer has been represented as an heroic figure, one who, like Brahm, is the moving and creative spirit of his world. The overtones of Genesis in the bridge-building descriptions also contribute to this notion. "With a sigh of contentment [he] saw that his work was good." Thus it is easy for Peroo to draw the conclusions he does about Findlayson's quick dismissal of the Gods. When Brahm wakes, the Gods die; when Findlayson wakes, the Gods die. In neither case can the "unreality" of the Indian deities survive the return of consciousness.

We have already commented on an alternative interpretation of this scene, the view that Findlayson forgets the Gods because his experience on the island has been such a traumatic one; because he has been cut down to size, has heard himself described as "dirt digging a little in the dirt" and cannot bear to confront this truth. "The great bridge to which Findlayson returns," Professor Tompkins writes, "seems a mirage floating on vapour."[16] Yet, there is nothing in the story to suggest that the bridge to which Findlayson returns after his night on the island

16. Tompkins, p. 192.

seems, or for that matter is, any less real than it was before the opium dream. Indeed, the one important fact we have about the bridge testifies to its absolute reality. For it has succeeded in subduing the Gods, has survived the unleashed fury of Mother Gunga. Moreover, if we are to believe Krishna, this victory is to be only the first of many which the bridge-builders will enjoy. "My people see their work," says the God who lives among men,

and go away thinking. They do not think of the Heavenly Ones altogether. They think of the fire-carriages and the other things that the bridge-builders have done, and when your priests thrust forward hands asking alms, they give unwillingly a little.

Thus Krishna's prediction confirms Peroo in his newly-acquired understanding of men like Findlayson, men who have only to awaken to annihilate the Gods.

It is true, of course, that the despairing doctrine of the Gods—"when Brahm ceases to dream, the heavens and the hells and the earth disappear . . ."—does have a certain validity. It is true, that is, that in one sense the universe is a meaningless and dream-like place in which all of man's actions prove ultimately futile and vain. What is more significant in this story, however, is Findlayson's attitude toward that doctrine. Miss Tompkins sees the engineer rejecting the position of the Gods on the theory that "it is necessary to man's health in this world that he should be shortsighted."[17] But this gives the Gods too much credit. It implies that they know a truth so terrible and so important that man does not dare confront it, when, in fact, the point of "The Bridge-Builders" is that the secret of the Gods is an inferior one, one that Findlayson has no diffi-

---

17. Tompkins, p. 193.

culty moving beyond, one which seems to him not so much
terrifying as irrelevant. It is in this sense that the Gods die
when Findlayson, through the hard work of reuniting body
and soul, awakens again to the reality of existence; they
are simply irrelevant in a human context.[18] Man, in other
words, need not trouble himself with the fact that the universe will someday be gone. He does not eat any less in the
morning because he knows that by evening he will be
hungry again, nor, except for special cases, does he deliberately choose oblivion today because tomorrow oblivion
will be forced upon him. Indeed, the Gods' prophecy of
ultimate annihilation, Findlayson well knows, so far from
rendering man's life meaningless, makes it more meaningful. The position is again the existentialist one. In an empty
universe, Kipling implies here, as he does in many of his
stories, man is nobody's creature and life is precious precisely because every moment of it is its own excuse for
being.[19]

But the key to this existentialist position is consciousness. In the words of Kierkegaard's famous aphorism, "To
shorten one's hours of sleep and buy up the hours of the
day and not to spare oneself, *and then to understand that
the whole is a jest*; aye, that is earnestness" (italics mine).
It is consciousness, then, not unconsciousness, which is
Findlayson's great weapon in life and the overwhelming
threat to the Gods. Indeed, throughout the story the Gods
are shown to exist only so long as Brahm sleeps; this they

18. When, for example, Findlayson speaks of his bridge as being
"pukka—permanent," he is not cherishing any illusions about his work
standing forever. He is using the term in the only way it can be used in-
telligibly by a human being, to mean unusually long-lasting.

19. See, in this connection, Walter Pater's "Conclusion" to *Studies in
the Renaissance*. Kipling, coming into prominence as he did in the London of the 1890's, would not have escaped the influence of this important
document.

have in common with man. But they also live only so long as *man* sleeps. They are the Gods of the opium eaters, of those who reject experience and seek oblivion in narcotics. They are "Gods of the jungle—names that the hunters of rats and noosers of dogs whisper in the thicket and among the caves," Gods of half-savage men who have not yet come into their legacy of consciousness.

It is this consciousness, Kipling says, that is the nemesis of the Gods. The beasts have always lived in fear of Brahm awakening, and now, Krishna warns them, they must face a more immediate threat. For man, too, can annihilate the Gods by awakening, and man has begun to stir. Findlayson, rousing himself from his drugged sleep, returns to a level of consciousness where the Gods cannot exist, where their glory is dimmed by the intenser light of reality. And the bridge that is the incarnation of that higher consciousness not only itself defeats the fading Powers but, as we have said before, also shows the way for other men to cross from "an old world of dying Gods to a new and freer life."

For bridge-building, as Kipling sees it in this story, is essentially educational. The day's work may produce certain material benefits even when it is performed unthinkingly. But it only becomes genuinely significant when it requires a man to confront reality on a high level of consciousness and teaches him respect for experience and for a life lived intensely and without deception. Thus for Hitchcock, Findlayson's young assistant, the process of building the bridge across the Ganges is also a process of achieving new awareness of the order and structure of life. "Gad, what a Cooper's Hill cub I was when I came on the works," the young man muses at one point, thinking back over three years of effort during which his struggles with the realities of stone and the realities of bureaucracy "had taught him power and responsibility."

Peroo, the third major character in "The Bridge-Builders," also emerges from his experiences with a fresh vision of life. Throughout the narrative, the native foreman is presented to us as a man struggling with the problem of divided loyalties, a man standing half-way across an unfinished bridge that links two worlds. Inevitably, he owes a certain allegiance to the old world of his childhood, the world of opium pellets and of that other opiate, the religion of the beast-Gods. Even when he is engrossed in the new and stimulating world of work, the pull of the old world is strong. The *guru* must be kept on and supported, even with all the doubts about his efficacy, the Gods must be propitiated with the proper ceremonies, and in moments of crisis the opium is there to dull the intensity of experience. "It is not good to look at death with a clear eye."

Yet for all his commitment to the old religion, it is plain that Peroo is even more strongly attracted to the new one and only awaits some crucial experience to confirm him in the decision he has already made. That new religion is not, of course, the Christianity which the bridge-builders have brought with them to India. Krishna makes this clear when he says "Their Gods! This is no question of their Gods—one or three—man or woman. The matter is with the people. *They* move and not the Gods of the bridge-builders." Indeed, the perfunctory formality of that religion is quite plain to the bridge-builders themselves. Findlayson, for example, thinks of how, at the completion of his work, "His Excellency the Viceroy would open the bridge in state, an archbishop would bless it, the first train-load of soldiers would come over it, and there would be speeches." And even Peroo, in his many skeptical moments, questions the Gods of Christianity as narrowly as he does his own.

Nevertheless, the bridge-builders' special vision of life has, for Peroo, something like the force of religion. It is not

the bridge itself—the material aspect of it—that attracts
him so much as what he calls the "honor" of the bridge, the
world view which the bridge implies and which makes his
impulsive prayer to the low-press cylinder not altogether
absurd. And though the native foreman's preference for
suspension bridges "that fly from bank to bank" and avoid
a direct confrontation with the river suggests that he may
still be looking for short cuts to power, Findlayson is nevertheless able to say to him, half seriously, "No matter, Peroo.
Another year thou wilt be able to build a bridge in thine
own fashion."

Yet, with all the preparation he has undergone for his
new life, Peroo still needs a clinching experience to convert
him once and for all. We know that he has already had experiences which were important steps along the road to his
conversion. Once, in the ship *Rewah*, for example, during
a storm at sea, he had been thrown forward by a wall of
water onto "the ring of the great black bow-anchor" and
found himself at the very brink of annihilation, "looking
down into those great deeps." In that moment, as he
clutched the ring, he was vouchsafed a memorable insight
into the nature of reality and oblivion, thinking, even in
the face of death, "If I lose hold I die, and [then] neither
the *Rewah* nor my place by the galley where the rice is
cooked, nor Bombay, nor Calcutta, nor even London, will
be any more for me."

The experience, as Peroo recalls it, is a powerful one.
Nevertheless, it remains for Findlayson to complete, in a
moment, the education to which many years and many
such events had contributed. The moment is one we have
already noted. The Chief Engineer, awaking from his
drugged sleep on the island, dismisses—easily but finally—
the whole world of Peroo's Gods, and does so simply by
returning to consciousness. The significance of the episode

is not lost on Peroo who, with typical directness, resolves on the spot to give his hitherto sacrosanct *guru* a sound thrashing.

iv

In 1890, *The Times* of London, editorializing about the young Anglo-Indian who had so recently and so spectacularly appeared on the literary scene, singled out "In the House of Suddhoo" for special mention. "That very grim story," *The Times* wrote, seems, together with two or three others, "to be almost the best of Mr. Kipling's writings, perhaps because [it appears] to lift the veil from a state of society so immeasurably different from our own."[20] *The Times* was only one of many publications to compliment Kipling for teaching his countrymen about India, for making quite clear and explicit what before had been obscure about the great sub-continent. It is ironic, then, to think how different from *The Times'* vision of them were Kipling's intentions when he wrote his early stories. For to the extent that the young author had any conscious didactic purpose at all in producing such a tale as "In the House of Suddhoo," that purpose was not to raise a veil but to lower one. The original audience for the story was, after all, Anglo-Indian, and its problem, therefore, was not total ignorance of India, but rather an unwarranted confidence in its limited knowledge of the country. Thus Kipling's educational object, in many of his early stories, was to shake his readers out of their smoking-room complacency, to insist upon the inscrutability of the land which the English took too much for granted; in short, to dramatize the fact that

20. Quoted by C. E. Carrington, *The Life of Rudyard Kipling* (New York, 1955), p. 155.

A stone's throw out on either hand
From that well-ordered road we tread,
And all the world is wild and strange. . .[21]

The picture of India, then, that emerges from such a
story as "In the House of Suddhoo" is not a clear-cut one.
Instead, it is an elusive image of an unfathomable land; an
image, in fact, rather akin to the shadowy figure of Azizun
—one moment a Lady of the City, the next a veiled woman,
irrecoverably lost among teeming millions and answering
no questions. Yet given such an image of India and given
the figure of the vain young narrator whom so many critics
sought to equate with Kipling himself, the theme of the
story emerges very clearly indeed. It is not a theme calculated to appeal to *The Times* of London, but it is one which
Kipling made use of several times in his early stories and
which George Orwell summed up in his phrase "the futility of the white man's dominion in the East."[22]

To find Kipling and Orwell on the same side of a colonial
question is not as odd as it may appear. (In a recent essay,
Richard Cook pointed out that the two men, having had
similar childhoods and similar experiences with the workings of empire, "shared a number of fundamental attitudes," and that "many of the qualities in Kipling to which
Orwell responded were basic to his own work."[23]) Indeed,
what seems much odder is to find the author of "In the
House of Suddhoo" and the author of "The Bridge-Builders" on such *different* sides of the same question. For no
two stories could be more completely opposed in their
views of British influence in the East.

---

21. These are the opening lines of the epigraph to "In the House of
Suddhoo."

22. George Orwell, "Shooting an Elephant," *Essays* (New York,
1954), p. 159.

23. Richard Cook, "Rudyard Kipling and George Orwell," *Modern
Fiction Studies*, VII (1961), 125.

L

We have already noted the sense of futility which
emerges from the depiction of imperialism in "Suddhoo."
In "The Bridge-Builders," on the other hand, to the extent
that Findlayson represents all creative Englishmen of good
will who went out to India in the days of empire, and to
the extent that Peroo represents all the promising Indian
natives, we see an example of Kipling's faith in the educational value of Britain's colonial experiment. True, commentators have often wondered whether Kipling might not
have been too uncritical about his country's imperialist
policies and too quick to accept the official propaganda
about educating the natives. Orwell, for example, accused
the author of failing to see empire as "primarily a money-
making concern," of failing to realize "that the map is
painted red chiefly in order that the coolie may be exploited."[24] But such an accusation cannot stand close scrutiny. First of all, the notion that Kipling was unaware of
the economic basis of empire cannot really be defended.
Such a story as "The Bridge-Builders" reveals that the author understood very well the economic function of the
proliferating railroads and bridges he so admired. Indeed,
it establishes the fact in a single passage, one in which
Ganesh, the God of money-lenders, explains to Mother
Gunga why he is quite content about the new bridge spanning the river. He has, Ganesh says, been studying his account-books over the shoulders of his clerks, and has seen
"that the names in the books are those of men in far places
. . . . [that] the money comes and goes swiftly, and the
account-books grow as fat as—myself."

Thus Kipling knew even before Orwell did that the
bridges and railroads being built in India were being built
to make money for men who were not Indians. But as an

---

24. Orwell, "Rudyard Kipling," *Essays*, pp. 126, 127.

on-the-spot witness of this building, what interested him
far more than its questionable motives was the fact that
under the noses of the investors, of the tycoons, indeed of
the British Government itself, the construction work was
producing something very different from the intended re-
sults. This, indeed, is the insight which is at the heart of
"The Bridge-Builders": that regardless of the grossly selfish
ends which a particular bridge may originally have been
designed to serve, the job it actually performs is to raise the
people who build it—through the very difficulty of the labor, the difficulty of transforming an idea into material
reality—from the condition of ignorance in which they can
be exploited to a position of strength and self-confidence
from which they can launch an attack on their exploiters.
The irony of colonialism is that it produces the conditions
for its own defeat, and it is this aspect of colonialism which
Kipling is in part dealing with in this story. Against the
background of such a story, Rupert Croft-Cooke's remark
about Kipling's respect for "government of the naturally
governable by the natural ruler" seems especially wide of
the mark. For Croft-Cooke's vision is obviously of a fixed
and unalterable social order, while Kipling clearly prophe-
sies, in a story like "The Bridge-Builders," what, in fact,
George Orwell was to live to see—an India powerful and
coherent enough to govern itself.

"The Bridge-Builders" is, then, a story in which Kipling
appears to be convinced of the efficacy of British colonialism, even as "In the House of Suddhoo" seems a gloomy
illustration of that "futility of the white man's dominion in
the East" which Orwell speaks of; and it is just such political inconsistency as this that has deeply troubled a number
of readers. Orwell himself never comments directly on such
discrepancies, though in his treatment of Kipling as a political thinker rather than as an artist he often criticizes by

implication the earlier author for failing to consider the political effects which his work as a whole might have on a reader. Sometimes this attitude of Orwell's is concealed in apparently straightforward statements. His remarks, for example, which we have already noted, "that Kipling does not seem to realize . . . that an empire is primarily a money-making concern" and "that the map is painted red chiefly in order that the coolie may be exploited," are a case in point.

The key words in these statements are "primarily" and "chiefly." Orwell knew, as a man who had seen colonialism up close, that now and then some good came of imperialist activities, and so—conscientiously—he added the qualifying adverbs to his remarks to be fair. Those qualifiers, however, are of further interest for what they imply about their author's standards of literary criticism. For since Orwell himself admits that imperialism occasionally has its creative moments, he can hardly be criticizing Kipling for writing about those moments. What he must be criticizing, then, is Kipling's failure to balance out the account, to show enough of the bad with the good either in the individual stories or in his work as a whole. And this, in turn, indicates that Orwell was applying to Kipling's works of fiction standards of judgment far more appropriate to, say, political essays.

It is the political essay which has an obligation to balance its accounts, to give all sides in a controversy a reasonably fair hearing. Orwell was himself always careful to fulfill this obligation. In "Shooting an Elephant," for example, speaking of his experiences as a colonial policeman in Burma, he says.

All I knew was that I was stuck between my hatred of the empire I served and my rage against the evil-spirited little beasts who tried to make my job impossible. With one part of my mind

I thought of the British Raj as an unbreakable tyranny . . .
with another part I thought that the greatest joy in the world
would be to drive a bayonet into a Buddhist's guts.[25]

The passage is an admirable one, direct, forceful and full of
that judicious weighing of contradictory opinions which
we expect to find in an Orwell essay. Indeed, Orwell would
no doubt have felt dishonest had he painted only one half
the picture without the other, and perhaps this accounts
for his insistence, implicit in his criticism of Kipling, that
all writers be as judicious and balanced as he.

But all writers are not essayists. Some write fiction, and
no fiction writer would worry for a moment about achieving the Orwellian sort of balance in his work. If there was
a story to be made out of the urge to bayonet a Buddhist
in the guts, that, for the artist, would be the only thing that
mattered. The companion piece, the story about the hatred
of imperialism, would have to wait till another day, and if
the proper plot or action failed to materialize, perhaps that
day would never come. But that would not matter. The
story about the Buddhist, supposing only that it was honestly imagined and well-written, would be enough. The
artist would have fulfilled his obligation to speak the truth,
not necessarily a statistical truth but one just as valid, a
truth about the nature of a particular experience.

In this light, perhaps, the inconsistency of "The Bridge-
Builders" and "In the House of Suddhoo" becomes less
important.[26] If Kipling had intended the body of his work
to be a coherent political system he would, we may suppose, have hesitated to include both of these stories in the

---

25. Orwell, "Shooting an Elephant," *Essays*, p. 155.
26. As Kipling remarked on another occasion, "I am consoled by the
thought that I am not the only person who has said one thing one day
and another the next." "The Classics and the Sciences," *A Book of Words*
(London, 1928), p. 251.

same edition of his writings for fear that his philosophy of imperialism might indeed seem "mindless." But he clearly had no such ambitions and therefore had no trouble making room in his complete works for the two tales. For him, each was sovereign in its own way and deserved to be read for itself, each had engendered the "flesh" most appropriate to its own nature, each displayed that internal order of its elements which is the only sort of consistency an artist need concern himself with.

This point cannot be made too strongly. As long as we think of Kipling's works as containing commentaries on colonialism *independent* of the stories and poems in which they appear—and it is the usual political approach to Kipling which forces us into that kind of thinking—we run into violent contradictions and the "mindlessness" of Trilling's accusation. But the moment we begin to read them in terms of their inner structures, read them as tales about particular human beings having unique experiences, most of the contradictions vanish. We have already seen that "The Bridge-Builders" is, in the last analysis, a story about the impact of Findlayson's work on Peroo. We may draw larger conclusions from this confrontation—indeed, those conclusions are there to be drawn—but however optimistic we may grow, on the basis of this story, about the efficacy of colonialism, we must agree that the political theory succeeds only insofar as Findlayson succeeds, that the real triumph is the triumph of a single man. By the same token, the white man's dominion, as it is ironically drawn for us in "In the House of Suddhoo," is futile only to the extent that the narrator of the story is futile and fails in his duty to himself.

It is when we attempt to discover the nature of that duty by examining these stories as works of art that we begin to sense the real consistency in Kipling's best work. For "The

Bridge-Builders" and "In the House of Suddhoo," diametri-
cally opposed as they are on the level of political commentary, both express the familiar Kipling vision of life which
we have encountered in so many other stories. It is a vision
based on the faith that consciousness and self-awareness
are life's real victories and that man's highest duty is to live
fully and, through his work in the world, to know that he
has lived. The narrator of "In the House of Suddhoo," like
Lieutenant Golightly, whom he resembles in many ways,
but also like Vickery and Helen Turrell, finds himself
trapped by events because he has failed to understand
them. Power must reside somewhere, and when, in his
ignorance, the young Englishman relinquishes control of
circumstances, circumstances begin to control him. Such
a figure as Findlayson, on the other hand, gains the limited
victory permitted him by virtue of a heightened consciousness achieved through hard labor. Findlayson triumphs by
insisting on the reality of experience and by embodying
that reality in work: for work, under which general heading comes the very special labor called imperialism, is to
Kipling a key metaphor, an act of almost religious intensity, perhaps the only religious act, the only incarnation
possible in an indifferent universe.

CHAPTER SIX ⬧

The Aesthetics of Violence

i

Orwell's joking depiction of the typical British colonialist
as "a *pukka sahib* in a pith helmet kicking a coolie" suggests, among other things, how intimately imperialism is
associated in most people's minds with brutality. And insofar as Kipling is best known to most readers as an apologist
for colonialism, his work has inevitably come to seem to
many a defense of brutality as well. Indeed, a reader may
know little else about Kipling, but he will be sure to have
heard of his reputation for condoning and even celebrating
gross violence in his poems and stories. As early as 1900,
Robert Buchanan was bitterly condemning Kipling as "the
voice of the hooligan,"[1] and more than forty years later,
George Orwell, equally harsh in his judgment of the writer,
declared that "there is not the slightest sign anywhere in
his work that he disapproves of [sadism and brutality]."[2]
Many other writers have made the same point just as vigorously. Richard Le Gallienne, for example, speaks of "Mr.
Kipling's genuine, unaffected love of brutality,"[3] and Max
Beerbohm, in his famous—if quite uncharacteristically viru-

---

1. Robert Buchanan and Sir Walter Besant, *The Voice of "The Hooligan": A Discussion of Kiplingism* (New York, 1900).

2. George Orwell, "Rudyard Kipling," *Essays* (New York, 1954), p.
124.

3. *Rudyard Kipling: A Criticism* (New York, 1900), p. 147.

lent—parody of Kipling in *A Christmas Garland*, mimics brilliantly not only the unique, jaunty style of his subject's verse and prose but also the pathological reveling in cruelty which, to Beerbohm, at any rate, seemed the chief distinguishing feature of Kipling's work.

> Then it's collar 'im tight, [Beerbohm wrote]
>   In the name o' the Lawd!
> 'Ustle 'im, shake 'im till 'e's sick!
>   Wot, 'e *would*, would 'e? Well,
>   Then yer've got ter give 'im 'Ell,
> An' it's trunch, trunch, truncheon does the trick.

Like much other criticism of Kipling, the charge of brutality can readily be substantiated. In volume after volume of Kipling's works the reader encounters incidents of bullying, beating, and rank sadism, acts of maliciousness most of which, it seems plain, the author is not merely reporting but is actually enjoying. Such an early story as "A Friend's Friend" from *Plain Tales From the Hills* is based upon one of the writer's favorite brutalities, the gang-up. The situation, familiar to Kipling *aficionados*, is one in which the members of an exclusive group combine to inflict excruciating mental and physical torture on an individual whose chief crime, for all anyone is able to tell, is being an outsider. It would be easy enough to dismiss this tale as one of its author's early mistakes were it not for the fact that as late as 1932, in *Limits and Renewals*, Kipling permitted the reprinting of a story of his called "The Tie," a work, similar in its outlines to "A Friend's Friend," in which group punishment is inflicted on the worst sort of outsider the writer can imagine, an insider gone bad.

And these pieces only mark the boundaries of Kipling's career. Repeatedly during the forty-five years which separate the two works the author returned to the device of the gang-up, and even in such a story as "The Village That

Voted the Earth Was Flat," often spoken of as one of Kipling's humorous best, the effect of all the great powers in England combining—to the obvious delight of the author—for the purpose of ruining a single village is far more grotesque and even sadistic than it is funny. Plainly, what these stories all have in common is the fact that brutality is not only their subject but also their object; that not content with merely contemplating sadism, they must *be* sadistic as well. Small wonder, then, that Kipling's voice should have come to be associated, in the minds of most people, with the voice of the hooligan.

But to condemn these particular works on the charge of brutality is not to condemn their author's output as a whole. Indeed, for every story in which we find Kipling delighting in the discomfort of his fellow creatures, there are many other tales in which human suffering is treated by the writer with respect and compassion. There can, for example, be nothing more brutal and senseless than the deaths of Ameera and her son in "Without Benefit of Clergy." Yet that brutality is clearly the brutality of the universe, and Kipling's necessary acceptance of such a universe only renders more poignant his pity for those who must suffer its cruelty. Bonamy Dobrée has spoken of compassion as the principal thread running through Kipling's work, has said of the author that "he symbolizes not hate, but a deep compassion; not malignant grandiosity and brute force, but humility, and tenderness amounting to deep pity,"[4] and he could hardly have gone so far were it not possible to make a real distinction, in most of the author's stories, between the brutality of their subjects and the compassion of the writer for the victims of that brutality. Thus if Kipling, in his poorest works, is sometimes per-

---

4.   Bonamy Dobrée, "Rudyard Kipling," *The Lamp and the Lute*, rev. ed. (London: 1964), p. 57.

sonally and vindictively violent, in his best fiction he depicts violence not to approve of it but to suggest, in terms of character and action, ways of meeting it, of overcoming it, and perhaps most important, of using it constructively.

There can be little doubt, for instance, that Kipling considered pain, violence and even brutality to be necessary elements in the creative process. That is to say, he conceived of art as emerging principally from the artist's intense awareness—his profound consciousness—of "things as they are," and for Kipling, to be aware of "things as they are" was to be aware largely of pain and violence. It is not difficult to understand why the author should have arrived at such a harsh vision of life; his every experience served to force such a philosophy upon him. Born into a loving and close-knit family, he found himself, at the age of six, suddenly separated from his parents and the only home he had ever known and made to live for more than five years in what he was always in later life to call "The House of Desolation." There he was brutalized by a hired "aunt" and "uncle," planned terrible but pathetically ineffectual revenges, and suffered alone the gradual deterioration of his sight. Even if we grant that the memory of an old man may exaggerate the injustices of youth, we can still see, in this early, inexplicable separation of the boy from parental affection, the origin of that "wound" of Kipling's which seemed, to Edmund Wilson[5] for one, so central to the later development of the artist.

Nor was this Kipling's only encounter with the cruel reality of life. Having survived the rigors of an English public school education, the young man, a startlingly mature seventeen, returned to the even more rigorous world of India, a world from which he was unexpectedly rescued by

---

5. Edmund Wilson, "The Kipling That Nobody Read," *The Wound and the Bow* (New York, 1947).

literary success at the age of twenty-five, just as earlier he
had been rescued from "The House of Desolation" by the
unexpected return of his mother to England. From his profound grief over the loss of his son in the First World War,
however, there was to be no rescue; no rescue, either, from
the physical agony which darkened and embittered his last
fifteen years. For Kipling, then, the "God of things as they
are" was to a large extent a cruel God.

But by definition, "things as they are" must be accepted;
to pretend that they don't exist is to reject life. Thus for
Kipling, life is always the consciousness of pain, and indeed in nothing so much as in this attitude is the author—
in his best work—to be seen as an artist rather than as the
political man he has appeared to be to so many commentators. For the response of the political man is, typically,
to move beyond the consciousness of pain to a consideration of how the world may be manipulated to ease the pain,
and it is to thoughts of such manipulation that he gives all
his energy. The artist, on the other hand, reserves his energy for the consciousness, the awareness, the act of contemplation itself.[6]

This mere acknowledgment of reality, however, does not
make a man an artist, nor does Kipling anywhere suggest
that it does. Though no one can be an artist *without* such
an acknowledgment, without devotion, for example, to the
gallingly intransigent material of his art, to the stubborn
physicality of his craft, such devotion is by its nature ma-
terialistic and thus egocentric and brutalizing. What Kip-

---

6. It is precisely when Kipling carries over his artistic temperament
into political matters that he gets into trouble. As Noel Annan has written
in "Kipling's Place in the History of Ideas," *Victorian Studies*, III (June
1960), 323-48, "Kipling lacked a gift, which greater writers possess, the
gift of understanding intuitively the [political] *consequences* of holding
a particular theory of human destiny. A Conservative must be aware of
the consequences of his creed: if he is not, he degenerates into a complacent defender of anything that actually exists."

ling sees is that at a certain point, the properly prepared craftsman, the man who has devoted himself truly to the contemplation of reality and who has suffered in the extreme the psychic pain attendant upon a deliberately cultivated awareness of "things as they are," can become the instrument of a force outside himself, a force which shapes his experience into art, transmuting the pain to beauty. This force, as it manifested itself in Kipling's own experience, the writer called—as D. H. Lawrence was later to call a similar force of his own—his Dæmon, a kind of inspiration whose comings and goings were not in his control but whose decisions he learned to trust implicitly. Thus, it is the movement of the artist from painful, self-centered contemplation of life to an almost Eastern surrender of the self, a yielding of the personality to superior external forces (a movement noted by Bonamy Dobrée in Kipling's own development from brutality to compassion), which lies at the heart of the author's aesthetic theory.

ii

This theory is nowhere directly stated by Kipling; it must be inferred from the stories and poems and from what little non-fiction the writer produced. In *A Book of Words*, for instance—an extremely guarded collection of brief after-dinner talks—one short essay, expansively entitled "Literature," offers a few bare hints of the author's ideas on the subject of his art. The 1,500-word piece makes the point that since writers have the job of recording the history of the "Tribe," and since for better or worse such records will be the only trace of the Tribe in centuries to come, the writer's job is the most crucial one in society and the one, therefore, most properly open to criticism and most dangerous. Later, it declares that all great writing is a miracle and that every Tribe gets the record it deserves. Here then, superficially stated, are all of the main elements of Kipling's aesthetic theory: the world of "things as they are," the danger and pain of contemplating such a world, and the miraculous nature of the skill that can transform this world into art. The posthumously published autobiographical memoir *Something of Myself* makes a number of these same points. There is a good deal of emphasis in the book on craftsmanship, on the sheer brutal difficulty of getting the job done, and there are, too, a number of references to the mysterious Dæmon, notably in the discussion of *Kim*, in which Lockwood Kipling, learning that his son's novel has been completed, asks "Did *it* stop, or you?" and on being told that "it was *It*," remarks "Then it oughtn't to be too bad."[7] But such tidbits can hardly be considered Jamesian musings on the craft of fiction, and for an understanding of Kipling's ideas about literature it is perhaps best to turn to the literature itself.

Especially in the stories he wrote about art, Kipling provides the reader with clues to his aesthetic theories and the part which violence plays in them. Such an early and artistically unsuccessful work as *The Light That Failed* (1891) is fairly rudimentary in its theorizing, but the central themes we have noted before are there. Painter Dick Heldar, instructing Maisie, warns her that "all we can do is to learn how to do our work, to be masters of our material instead of servants, and never to be afraid of anything," and then goes on to explain that "good work has nothing to do with—doesn't belong to—the person who does it. It's put into him or her from outside." Again, the Dæmon and the pain of mastering the physical world.

In other, later tales these ideas play more important roles, conspicuously in such works as "Wireless," "The Eye

---

7. *Something of Myself*, p. 150.

of Allah," "Dayspring Mishandled," and "The Bull That Thought," all, in one way or another, narratives about art and the artist. "Wireless" (1904) is a perhaps too-clever science-fiction or fantasy story which nevertheless offers a powerful insight into Kipling's harsh aesthetic. The setting of the tale is a druggist's shop at the rear of which an early wireless experiment is being conducted. A receiving set has been tuned so as to vibrate exactly to the wavelength of a signal originating at a great distance, a signal which races around the earth in search of an instrument capable of giving it a voice. Meanwhile, at the front of the shop, another kind of wireless experiment is in progress. Young Mr. Shaynor, a tubercular pharmicist's assistant, is huddled for warmth near the stove as freezing gusts howl in from the sea. He has just returned from a walk with his sweetheart, Fanny Brand, and wracked with the pain which the icy winds have brought, he has accepted the offer of a soothing drink, concocted by the narrator from miscellaneous syrups and elixirs. Now, drugged by the medicine and temporarily released from his own personality, he becomes himself a kind of receiving set, a set tuned, by the accidents of his life and this particular evening, to the supernal wavelength of the Keatsian Dæmon, and he begins to set down, painfully and with a number of distortions, lines from "The Eve of St. Agnes." When Shaynor awakens, it is determined that he has never read any Keats, and so the narrator is able to formulate a theory of artistic inspiration which sees the poet as a kind of receiving set that can be tuned by varying experiences to varying "wavelengths," and inspiration itself as the radio waves searching for an instrument that will, with its own energy, amplify the weak broadcast signal. Since "like causes *must* beget like effects," Shaynor, some of whose experiences have been similar to Keats's, is able to write poetry something like Keats's.

The story is perhaps a little too clever to be wholly satisfying, but if we ignore the elaborate pseudo-scientific explanations and comparisons, there still remains Kipling's
clear statement of what is required for a man to become
sensitive to the Dæmon of inspiration. During the course
of the story we are repeatedly made aware of the fact that
Shaynor is in pain. He suffers, and suffers greatly, the pangs
of illness, of freezing cold and, not least significant of all,
the violent pangs of love. And it is the intensity of his pain
which, more than anything else, raises him to the energy
level at which he is capable of amplifying the signals of
the Dæmon. It is significant that while Shaynor's verses
are something like Keats's, they are not identical with them
—are, in fact, less precise and sometimes rather vulgar. This
is because Shaynor is a coarser man than the poet, a man of
less heightened sensibility who lives at a considerably
lower level of consciousness. Thus, if Keats wrote poetry
more exquisitely beautiful than Shaynor's, it is because—
Kipling implies—he was capable of more exquisite suffering. The beauty is a direct function of the pain.

"The Eye of Allah" (1926) also emphasizes the relationship between art and pain. John of Burgos, a medieval il-
luminator of manuscripts, is able to reproduce, with terrifying accuracy and beauty, the looks on the faces of the
sick and the possessed. We soon learn, however, that his
mastery has been acquired only at great cost, for at least
one of the faces on which his artist's conscience had forced
him to bend his full artist's consciousness was that of his
dying and much-beloved wife. Out of the pain of intense
and, for him, inescapable contemplations like these came
drawings of such poignancy and horror—including repro-
ductions of the tiny life forms he discovered with the aid
of a primitive microscope—that they could only, according
to one observer, have been the products of a drugged mind.

But at this suggestion that great art might conceivably result from anything but the clearest, highest and most painful consciousness of reality, John of Burgos rebels. "In *my*
craft," he says with finality, "we dare not drug. It kills hand
and eye. My shapes are to be seen honestly, in nature."

The late story "Dayspring Mishandled" (1932), a product of Kipling's sixties, seems, at first glance, typical of the
savage revenge tales which have given the author such a
bad name, but on a careful reading it appears, instead, to
be one more illustration of the part which—according to
Kipling—brutality plays in the creative process. Castorley,
careless and insensitive, has casually blackened the name
of a good woman and has made a mortal enemy of Manallace. The latter, seeking some enormous and appropriate
revenge, considers that his enemy is a fairly talented and
rising Chaucer scholar and hatches a plot that will destroy
the man's career and break his heart. Inspired by a hate
which the reader is invited to share, or at least to approve
of, Manallace first composes a "lost" poem of Chaucer's
(he is skillful at such parody), and then, over a period of
years devoted to pure craftsmanship, painfully learns all
that he must know about inks and papers and so on to be
able to produce a convincing forgery. Next, having cleverly
brought the "new" poem to the attention of Castorley, he
hires on as the man's assistant in order to help prepare the
great critical and scholarly masterpiece which will first
raise his enemy to the heights and will later, at the appropriate moment, be the instrument of his destruction.
But then an astonishing thing happens. When the moment
arrives for the trap to be sprung, Manallace finds himself
incapable of springing it. The meaning of this strange
paralysis soon becomes clear. For years, the great revenge
plot has been drawing for creative energy upon Manallace's intense and seemingly inexhaustible supply of hatred,

M

and has slowly and secretly been transmuting that hatred into the cool, impersonal perfection of a work of art. Thus, when the moment for revenge arrives, Manallace discovers that there is not enough hatred left in him to spring the trap, that in fact the feeling he now has for the ailing Castorley is not bitterness but compassion. As a final irony, the secret avenger must now spend all his time protecting his work of art, all his energy preventing his hoax from being revealed by Castorley's wife, another hater, but one who has had no creative outlet for her violent energy.

iii

Of the hundreds of stories that Kipling wrote, the one which most fully explores the relationship of brutality to art is "The Bull that Thought" (1926), a moving yet delightful tale, in which the part of the artist is played by an amazingly precocious animal. That it should have occurred to Kipling to employ a bull as a symbol of the artist may call for some explanation. Of course, there is ample precedent in the writer's own stories for the metaphoric use of animals. "A Walking Delegate," "The Maltese Cat," "Below the Mill Dam," "The Bridge-Builders," and especially the tales in *The Jungle Books* are all works in which animals, by confronting the world on their own terms, help to illuminate the experiences of men. Nor has the technique died out among serious modern writers. Liam O'Flaherty in Ireland and Walter Van Tilburg Clark in America, for example, have both produced good stories in this genre.

As it is used in Kipling's tale, this metaphoric technique has the virtues and drawbacks of any analogy. One virtue of the comparison between the creative spirit and the fighting bull is that it calls our attention, in a deliberately fanciful and therefore a memorable way, to certain universal characteristics of the artist which Kipling did not think it possible to illuminate so well in more conventional terms. In particular, the actions of the bull permit the author to make the point that at the heart of even the most delicate creative act is a brutal, primal energy, and to emphasize the extent to which creativity is a function of that violent, often destructive force.

The chief drawback of the metaphor, on the other hand, is the ever-present danger of misinterpretation, for the very audacity of the comparison requires that we exercise some imagination in translating the actions of the bull into human terms. When, for example, Apis cleans his horns in the earth after one of his murders, we must see in his fastidiousness the narcissistic self-absorption of the artist, his preoccupation with his tools and techniques at the expense of personal relations. To imagine that Kipling is trying to say, in this episode, that all artists are concerned with cleanliness and good appearance is to be overly literal. It was surely no part of the author's intention to suggest that —in the words of one critic[8]—Pontius Pilate would have made a good artist because he washed his hands.

A second potential drawback of the bull-artist analogy is that a story founded on it may at any moment lapse into a grotesque "portrait of the artist as a young bull"—which Kipling's story in fact does. But because the author was aware of the comic possibilities inherent in his metaphor, he was able to exploit them at every turn, wasting no opportunity for humorous irony. Apis, we are told, "being a genius . . . extemporizes with the materials at hand," he is "the Cyrano of the Camarque," "the Master, wearied after a strenuous hour in the atelier, unbuttoned and at ease with some not inexpert but limited disciple." Thus Kipling—like Apis, at ease and unbuttoned—takes full advantage of the

---

8. Robert M. Adams, in correspondence.

grotesqueness of his metaphor, directing his narrative toward its comic climax, toward what C. A. Bodelsen has described as the stage of "cosmic mirth"[9] which occurs in so many of Kipling's stories and which always characterizes there the moment of creative fulfillment.

We are not being overly fanciful when we consider "The Bull that Thought" a history of the artist, for though the use of bullfighting as a metaphor for art was not as inevitable in Kipling's day as it is in our own (*The Sun Also Rises*, for example, had been out only a year when "The Bull that Thought" made its appearance in *Debits and Credits*), there can be no doubt that the author intended his tale to be a study of art and the artist. Those two key words appear again and again in the text, references to the other arts abound, and perhaps most important, the opening pages of the story establish the special aesthetic terms in which we are to see and judge the rest of the narrative.[10]

Like "Mrs. Bathurst," "The Bull that Thought" makes use of the picture-frame, a device for presenting stories as if they were actually being told to the author by participants in the action. In the hands of some writers, the picture-frame is little more than a formalized way of getting a story started, complete with listeners taking their ease in the smoking-room, lighted cigars, replenished drinks and

---

9. See "The Revelation of Mirth," *Aspects of Kipling's Art* (New York, 1964), pp. 1-28. See also J. M. S. Tompkins, "Laughter," *The Art of Rudyard Kipling* (London, 1959), pp. 33-54, and Bonamy Dobrée, "Laughter," *Rudyard Kipling: Realist and Fabulist* (London, 1967), pp. 37-43.

10. In his essay on "The Bull that Thought" in *Aspects of Kipling's Art*, C. A. Bodelsen discusses some of the same matters that I do in the present chapter, though we arrived at our interpretations independently and have placed our emphasis differently. On occasion, the two studies disagree, but rather than turn my own chapter into a detailed commentary on Professor Bodelsen's, I simply commend his excellent essay to the reader's attention.

unobtrusive servants poking up the fire. Not so in Kipling's best stories. In these, the picture-frame elements are invariably significant, contributing to the structures of the tales and helping to establish their themes. In "Mrs. Bathurst," for example, we have noted the importance of the bantering early pages and of the apparently irrelevant anecdote about Boy Niven in readying us for the later revelations about Vickery's fate. "The Bull that Thought" has a similarly meaningful opening, an opening which introduces the story's discussion of art and which prepares the way for the appearance of Apis, the wonderful thinking bull.

The initial episode in the introductory portion of the tale is the automobile time-trial, a seemingly pointless digression which is, in reality, the first of many metaphors for art in the story. In the big ungainly-looking touring car we have an image of brute power, exquisitely controlled. (Both the brutality and the control are essential to art, as Kipling shows in this story and as we shall note in a moment.) And in the perfect conditions of weather and road that make the trial possible, we have an instance of that "confederate season" upon which all greatness must wait. Tremendous power under precise control at an auspicious moment—these are some of the elements in Kipling's definition of art. But there is more to the definition than that, and the narrative's second episode adds, to the images of craftsmanship represented by the car, a note of the mystical. That episode involves the drinking of M. Voiron's champagne, a wine composed, Kipling tells us, "of the whispers of angels' wings, the breath of Eden and the foam and pulse of Youth renewed." The phrases are extravagant ones but they are obviously chosen to convey the unique magic of the champagne, a champagne which is as far above ordinary wines as art is above the pedestrian accomplishments of ordinary men. Taking all these elements together, then —brute power, exquisite control and a touch of the miraculous—we have the essence of art as Kipling saw it in "The Bull that Thought."

These metaphors for art in the first few pages of the story are closely related to similar elements in the body of the tale. The automobile, for example, appearing in the opening scene as an image of controlled power, recurs frequently in the course of the narrative in conjunction with the bulls, themselves symbols of potentially creative energy. One instance of such association occurs as early as the second sentence of the story where, before we know the function or significance of either automobile or bull, we find the two linked in the narrator's explanation that the repeated postponements of the automobile time trial are the result of the "unchancy cattle" of the district. Later, listening to M. Voiron talk about his intelligent animals, we learn that they "graze and they ruminate, by choice, facing our Mistral, which is more than some automobiles will do." And still further along we encounter a passage in which Apis, the thinking bull, is described as coming to a dead stop "like a car with four brakes." Kipling was, of course, far too conscious an artist for these repeated parallels to be accidental. Thus when we discover that the culmination of the art of champagne at the beginning of the story and of the art of bullfighting at the end are both to be understood in terms of reawakened youth—the wine being described as composed of the "pulse of youth renewed," and Chisto pictured as so inspired that "his youth returned to that meritorious beef-sticker—the desire, the grace and the beauty of his early dreams"—we should be ready to grant that in "The Bull that Thought" Kipling was primarily concerned with producing a study of art and the artist.

Indeed, the story of Apis is nothing less than the classic

story of the artist's growth—a kind of bovine *bildungsro-man.* As the tale begins, the calf who is to develop into "the bull that thought" is "an infant indistinguishable from his companions," just as the disguised motor car seems insignificant at first to M. Voiron. Soon, however, falling sick, he is set apart from the others and is taken into the big home farmyard where he has an opportunity to acquire an education that is available to none of his contemporaries. The education involves pitting himself against the children who come to practice their bullfighting on him, involves a constant training, the repeated bringing into play of every source of strength at his command.

Apis thrives on this regimen of constant challenge, and given his remarkable natural endowments—his name suggests the Egyptian bull-god of creativity—he is soon amazing everyone. Like a good artist, he learns to work with the materials that are at hand, using them in brilliant combinations to create astounding effects, and he never forgets a lesson once he has learned it. He is never deceived by appearances either, but invariably sees to the heart of a problem or into the mind of an opponent, and thus has the incalculable advantage of dealing always with reality. "Have you seen," we are told, "that he is not deceived by the jacket when the boy waves it? He uses it to find the boy." Finally, he is totally amoral and more than a little brutal. His one concern is the achievement of perfection in his art, and to reach his goal he will employ any method that works. He will cheat and betray, and it is not surprising that one of his most formidable weapons is the wholly unexpected and overwhelmingly effective "side-kick."

Later, turned out onto the grazing land and in the practice bullring at Arles, Apis participates in the second phase of his education; having learned his basic skills, he is now ready to perfect them. Naturally, his contemporaries are no match for him. Unscrupulously, but wholly without shame, Apis murders one after another of his less intelligent brothers, deceiving them, rushing at them "at dusk, from the ambush of a wind-break," knocking them over and disembowelling them "by an oblique charge from behind." Such vicious behavior is, of course, extremely significant for conveying Kipling's vision of the young artist's egotism and violent competitiveness. Still more telling, however, is the fact that at the conclusion of each performance, the murderer withdraws a little from the victim, kneels down, and carefully cleans his horns in the earth. This devastating fastidiousness, the author clearly means us to see—terrible yet admirable—is the authentic mark of the true artist, of one more concerned with aesthetics than ethics, more dedicated to the beautiful than to the good.

Called back to the home farmyard for further training and then sent on to Arles for final polishing, Apis at first displays the sense of humor that he has in common with "so many natural murderers. One knows the type among beasts as well as among men. It possesses a curious truculent mirth—almost indecent but infallibly significant."[11] He permits his now deadly horns to be padded, and he moves brilliantly through the steps of the *corrida*, always in control but always reserving the final, fatal surge. Even so, when he is asked to repeat himself, "which no true artist will tolerate," Apis kneels to rub the padding from his horns and then, as everyone flees from the ring and from the challenge of this consummate craftsman, the thinking bull faces the dilemma which sooner or later presents itself to all great artists. Having achieved the "breadth of technique that comes of seasoned art, and, above all, the passion that arrives after experience," Apis, watching the

---

11. Kipling might almost be describing here the kind of violent humor we find in many of his own stories.

whole world rushing from him in that panic which is a tribute to his mastery, confronts the nearly impossible task of finding a subject worthy of his genius.

The solution of this problem, waiting in the bullring of a small Catalan town on the road to Barcelona, forms the triumphant finale of "The Bull that Thought." For a while, Apis, though participating at last in a real bullfight, his horns unpadded and his life at stake, is betrayed by his superb craftsmanship into the usual easy round of meaningless victories. Drawing upon all the experiences of his youth and all the cunning of his maturity, he has no difficulty in destroying his opponents. His triumphs, however, are empty ones, and in a short time he finds himself alone in the middle of the ring, not yet having been truly challenged and now at the crisis of his artistic life.

It is at this point in the story that Kipling's insight into the nature of art becomes most interesting. Apis "had now involved himself in a stupendous drama of which he only could supply the third act. And, except for an audience on the razor-edge of emotion, he had exhausted his material." The bull had gone as far as craftsmanship could take him, and now he was beginning to see that as yet he had gone nowhere at all. With his great brutal power under superb control he, like the motor car in the automobile time-trial at the beginning of the story, had outdistanced all his opponents, indeed, had literally destroyed them. Yet thus far their deaths had been the only products of his violent genius, and the only possible product of death was more death. Apis, standing alone in the middle of the bullring, could perhaps sense the four or five Civil Guards "fingering the breeches of their rifles . . . waiting for the word from the Mayor to fire on him."

What was missing from the display, then, what had been missing all along, was a spark of the dæmonic (represented by the miraculous champagne early in the tale), that indispensable ingredient of true art which alone can defeat death. Here Apis' vision becomes almost metaphysical. For the bull now seems to understand that as long as he uses his talent as an instrument for destroying his opponents, as long as he places his genius at the service of purely personal survival, he is moving inevitably toward isolation and death. Only when he turns his abilities to a creative act, he recognizes, "with the detachment of the true artist who knows he is but the vessel of an emotion from whence others, not he, must drink," will he be able to receive life in the act of giving it.[12]

Apis' ultimate creation, his masterpiece, so to speak, is Chisto, the mediocre bullfighter become momentarily great. Chisto, advancing on the bull when the other matadors hesitate to accept the animal's challenge, awakens, with his courage and his herdsman's knowledgeable competence, all that is most creative in Apis; here at last is a subject worthy of the bull's genius. It must be emphasized, however, that Chisto is Apis' subject. The reader's experience with bullfights, in art or in actuality, might lead him to suppose that the relationship between the two would be just the other way around, but Kipling makes it plain that Apis is in control of events at every moment.

This is not to say that Chisto brings nothing to the performance. If he is shown to be Apis' subject, the bull's own creation, he is also described as "at heart" an artist, "a not inexpert if limited disciple," and there is no contradiction here. Every artist must have the proper materials to work with and must have them at the proper moment if he is

---

12.   In chapter seven of *The Light that Failed*, Kipling makes essentially this same point, having Dick tell Maisie that "the instant we begin to think about success and the effect of our work—to play with one eye on the gallery—we lose power and touch and everything else. . . . If we make light of our work by using it for our own ends, our work will make light of us, and, as we're the weaker, we shall suffer."

to do his best. The motor car at the beginning of the story triumphs because it has found the right road and the right night. Apis triumphs, escapes death at the hands of the Civil Guards, only because chance has brought to the bull-ring at the crucial moment the perfect material for the thinking bull's art: Chisto, the herdsman—inspiring, self-effacing, sympathetic, and—most important for the material of art—responsive to creativity. All great artists leave two legacies, their works and their influence. Chisto, at the moment he steps into the arena, is both the work of art which Apis will create and the disciple he will make, and with his appearance what Kipling calls the third act of the drama is conceived.

It is an act of highest art, rooted firmly in the craftsman-like skill which the animal has been developing all its life, but now heightened by a special creative impetus. Apis, in full charge of the moment, undertakes to revive the fading dream of an aging matador, and in conferring new life upon the man, in the paradoxical manner of art, receives his own life in return. Slowly and hypnotically, or else grotesquely "relaxing into pure buffoonery," the two flow about one another, arousing in the watchers first awe and then delighted laughter, that "cosmic mirth" which appears in such other Kipling stories as "My Sunday at Home" and "The Miracle of St. Jubanus," and which, as we have seen, always represents there the final touch of healing, the release of the self, the return to life. For submerging themselves in their art, abandoning themselves to restorative hilarity, Apis and Chisto achieve an immortality they could never have won with mere egotistical displays of skill. It is not given to many bulls to leave the arena alive, nor is it given to many artists to achieve immortality,[13] to go out by the same door through which they entered. But when Apis and Chisto have finished their per-

---

13. In the essay "Fiction," Kipling sets the number rather low. "Quite

formance, they leave the ring together, and Kipling's parable of the growth of the artist through violence is complete.

iv

No subject can be more personal or more immediate for an artist than the subject of his art, and it is therefore not surprising to find Kipling drawing heavily and repeatedly on his own experiences in "The Bull that Thought." Indeed, the history of Apis, the·artist among bulls, goes so far as to reflect a number of specific incidents in the author's own life. When quite young, for example, Kipling, like Apis, had an infirmity—his failing vision—which set him apart somewhat from his contemporaries and inevitably threw him back on his own resources. Again, like Apis, Kipling grew up in unusual surroundings which he cultivated assiduously and which were later to constitute the basis and sometimes the actual material of his art. (Apis takes advantage of the carts and tractors in the farmyard when he is learning his art, and in their absence, in the small Catalan arena, he improvises with the bodies of horses and men.) And finally, like the miraculous thinking bull, the young author was destined to be turned out early into the world to try his strength with his peers. In these and in many other ways the two artists—man and animal—seem strikingly alike.

In spite of these parallels, however, it would be wrong to hunt for clues to Kipling biography in "The Bull that Thought," or to think of the tale as primarily a veiled memoir or confession. For if the incidents in the narrative seem to echo events in the author's personal history, they

a dozen writers," he says, "have achieved immortality in the past 2,500 years." *A Book of Words*, p. 283.

also suggest, in a stylized way, the pattern of nearly every artist's life. Thus what is, for students of Kipling, just as significant about this story as its autobiographical over- tones is the fact that it embodies, in a remarkably coherent structure and in what appears to be virtually final form, the author's own mature conception of art. Since no other state- ment so serious or so complete exists of Kipling's aesthetic theories, "The Bull that Thought" automatically becomes a document of some importance for shedding light on ques- tions which have frequently been raised about the author and his work but which seldom have had satisfactory answers.

The very title of the work, for example, introduces a theme which we have already had occasion to see is central to Kipling's vision of life. The story is called "The Bull that Thought," and Bonamy Dobrée, paraphrasing one of Kip- ling's most persistent ideas, has written that "it is thought which produces the only action worth while."[14] The word "thought" is, we know, especially when it is used in connec- tion with Kipling, an ambiguous one, and to the extent that it implies cerebration and cerebration only—that is, the comparatively limited exercise of the rational faculty— it seems almost anti-artistic in its effect. Indeed, emphasis upon thought in this narrow sense has been, through the years, responsible for much of the distortion in Kipling criticism; we have already seen how often the author has been dealt with as a political thinker or a social commen- tator and how seldom as an artist. In part, Kipling was him- self responsible for having this reputation. So many of his verses are hardly more than cleverly rhymed aphorisms, so many of his poorer tales seem to be tracts rather than stories, that we are not wholly surprised when we find a

---

14. *Kipling Journal* (December 1940), 21.

critic discussing the author's ideas while ignoring their expression.

More than that, emphasis upon thought in art—to the extent that thought implies a fairly pedestrian application of the mind to problem-solving—also suggests a certain distrust of the mystical, the intuitive, and the purely aesthetic in life and a corresponding celebration of craftsmanship and professionalism. Of course, all art must be based upon sound craftsmanship, and professionalism, insofar as it implies solid competence and a continuity of effort, is also desirable. Nevertheless, most artists and critics would agree that craftsmanship and professionalism are too limited and too mechanical, by themselves, to produce great art, that the creative act does not fall solely within the province of the rational.

If, then, Kipling really considered thought, in its narrow, almost utilitarian sense, to be the central principle of art, he seems once again to have been on the wrong side of the debate about aesthetics—especially in the eighteen-nineties —and once again he himself is largely to blame for his bad reputation. For it is he who dedicated so many of his stories and poems to the thoughtful and painstaking builders and engineers of the world and to their clever manipulation of mechanical detail and their patient, unspectacular putting of one foot before the other. It is he who chose always to talk shop about his craft instead of discussing seriously the mystery of his art. And it is he who created, in the young journalist of so many of the tales, the image of the artist as an intelligent, self-conscious man of words at the service of the inarticulate, intuitive man of action. Under these circumstances, we can hardly wonder at Kipling's reputation as an extremely clever and competent verse technician and story-teller whose rough-and-ready, business-like approach to his work and apparent distrust of poetic flights proclaim him an artisan of the first rank but not an artist. Nor can we wonder that the designation of Apis, the artist among beasts, as the bull that "thought" seems to reiterate the narrowness of the author's aesthetic vision. For though thinking is miraculous in a beast, in an artist mere thought implies a kind of limitation.

Kipling's definition of thought, however, was a good deal more comprehensive than we have suggested thus far, and his ideas about art and the artist were not limited to notions of mere cleverness or even of craftsmanship. Indeed, if "The Bull that Thought" says anything at all, it says that cleverness and craftsmanship cannot by themselves produce truly great art. The whole of Apis' struggle to achieve "immortality" makes this point. Throughout the tale it is the animal's specially heightened consciousness, his ability always to see through to the reality of an experience which gives him the crucial edge over each of his opponents, man or beast. "He pursued, you understand, the person, not the propaganda," Kipling tells us, and toward the end of the story when Apis, "interrogating the Devils themselves upon their secrets," seems to be saying impatiently, "Yes, I know that—and *that*—and *that*! Tell me more—more!" it is plain that what he is seeking is not more technique, but rather something beyond technique, a different kind of knowledge, a higher order of consciousness, an intenser vision of reality. Thoreau once wrote, "Be it life or death, we crave only reality. If we are really dying, let us hear the rattle in our throats and feel cold in the extremities; if we are alive, let us go about our business." There is something of this fervor in every artist's pursuit of the truth, and it is toward the realization of such a truth that Apis' "thought" is chiefly directed. We have encountered before in Kipling's fiction the notion of heightened consciousness as man's ultimate resource, notably in such works as "Without

Benefit of Clergy" and "The Bridge-Builders." But in "The Bull that Thought" we find consciousness very clearly designated as the principle attribute of the artist, and art criticism, therefore, defined—in the words of the story— as the study of "what a beast who thinks can achieve."

v

Consciousness of reality, however, frequently means— as we have already noted and as the Thoreau quotation, for example, makes clear—awareness of the harsh and brutal in life, and it is plain from even a brief synopsis of "The Bull that Thought" that one of the story's most important ingredients is brutality. Indeed, as we have already suggested, Kipling seems to have chosen a bull as his metaphor for the artist precisely because of the opportunity it would give him to introduce violence into his narrative. Again and again Apis' cruelty, even his treachery, are called to our attention. The bull is spoken of as a Minotaur, an Apache who shamelessly disembowels rival bulls and who, participating in his first real bullfight, almost casually murders three men. More than anything else, it is these murders that raise the perennial issue of Kipling's brutality. True, death is something that happens at bullfights and is not an invention of Kipling's; true, these are fairly blood-less executions of faceless people, straw men who are never presented as individuals, whose very anonymity takes some of the curse off their deaths, and whose destruction is never shown to give anyone pleasure. But still, these killings seem to some readers an uncalled-for extravagance, another instance of Kipling the sadist taking over from Kipling the artist. Are they, after all, necessary?

Simply in mechanical terms, in terms of plot structure, the deaths at the end of "The Bull that Thought" *are* necessary; the climax of the story demands the violence which the author has supplied. What, for example, would be the meaning of Chisto's courageous gesture if it were not made in the face of almost certain death? What would be the significance of Apis' triumph if that triumph were not literally snatched from the jaws of annihilation? We have only to raise these questions to see the answers, to realize that the relief and pleasure we feel at the story's final scene we feel precisely because Chisto and Apis do their dance of life in the presence of death, a presence which is, in fact, essential if the story is to have any serious meaning at all.

Yet the violence in the last pages of "The Bull that Thought" performs something more than a simple mechanical function; like much of Kipling's violence, it is central to the author's intention in the tale, to the story's moral and aesthetic implications. Every shock of life had taught Kipling—and every experience with his art had confirmed him in the faith—that men achieve greatness not in spite of, but rather because of, the powerful opposition they meet with in a cruelly haphazard world. (The story takes place in the aftermath of the first World War, and the absurdity and violence of that conflict are always at the back of the narrator's mind.) Thus, time and again, in his stories and poems, the author found metaphors to depict victory as a function of defeat, success as an outgrowth of failure, life as a product of death; to show the flower of safety—in Hotspur's terms—being plucked, at great risk, from the nettle of danger. In "The Hymn of the Breaking Strain," for instance, a man, pressed to the end of his endurance, finds in his failure—and in the knowledge of failure—his only hope of triumph. Again, in the story "Uncovenanted Mercies," taken from a volume significantly titled *Limits and Renewals*, Azrael, the Angel of Death, says, "I've seen wonderful work done—with My Sword practically at people's throats," to which Satan adds, "Let's take Job's case. *He* didn't reach the top of his form, as your people say, until I had handled

N

him a little." And in "The Bull that Thought," Apis and Chisto achieve their success only when they too are threatened with death, Apis by the guns of the *Guardia* and Chisto by the horns of Apis.

Such a threat, very far from being a sadistic whim on Kipling's part, is for the author the most necessary experience of life, the penultimate reality of the world. (Only the victory snatched from death is more real.) But for death to be able to yield up life, for it to be productive of anything but more death, it must first of all be seen and accepted for what it is; the reality of it must be confronted without fear. Such a confrontation is genuinely rare. Most men choose, in one way or another, to deny the fact of death and, in denying it, to give up all hope of wresting life from it. The denials may take many forms. In "The Bull that Thought," for example, as in "Without Benefit of Clergy," the clear-eyed acceptance of the reality of death by such figures as Apis and Ameera is sharply contrasted with the retreat into ritual which is the response of other characters in the stories. We have already noted how self-defeating ritual is in an India burdened with famine and plague. Now Kipling shows us that it is just as useless in the pastures and bull-rings of France and Spain.

There are several references in "The Bull that Thought" to rituals and their futility. The ceremonial of the keys at the bull-ring, for example, designed to predict the outcome of the afternoon, fails even to suggest to the spectators what is really to happen. Again, the whole structure of the bull-fight, with its complex order of events and its elaborate customs, is discredited by the reality of Apis' brilliance and creativity. And perhaps most suggestive of the inadequacy of ritual, the reaction of Christophe, the herdsman, to Apis' first murder is to sprinkle some holy water over the bull, whom, we are archly told, it does not affect. We would, of course, hardly expect such a gesture to affect Apis. With his talent for pursuing "the person, not the propaganda," with his contemptuous dismissal of mere reputation in favor of honest skill—he curtly and permanently explodes the myth of Villamarte (the rival bull-fighter) while cleverly developing all of Chisto's possibilities—it is clear that he is wholly given over to reality. He is a bull that thinks, a bull whose chief weapon is consciousness.

But such commitment to "things as they are," we are shown, can involve great risks; reality is often brutal, and sometimes the near approach to it can be fatal. This is, of course, what Kipling meant when, in "Literature," he spoke of art as being the most "dangerous" of all occupations. It is dangerous in two ways. First, it is a threat to the complacent society which does not appreciate how perfect and how reckless is the artist's commitment to reality and to the techniques for achieving reality. Thus Apis, challenged to repeat himself in the home farmyard, as if his performance had been something learned by rote and not a unique expression of himself, turns on the spectators: "He had rubbed the pads off his horns. Then he rose, dancing on those wonderful feet that twinkled, and he said: 'Now, my friends, the buttons are off the foils. Who begins?' We understood. We finished at once." This concept of the artist as a menace to ordinary society differs emphatically from the eighteenth-century view of the poet as one who simply formulates a consensus—"What oft was thought, but ne'er so well expressed." Rather, it is a distinctly Romantic idea, exemplified, for instance, by the "dangerous" seer of Coleridge's

> Weave a circle round him thrice,
> And close your eyes with holy dread,
> For he on honey-dew hath fed,
> And drunk the milk of Paradise.

N*

This Romantic vision persisted at the heart of the Aesthetic Movement and, with its insistence on the supremacy of art, profoundly influenced Kipling's ideas, though the writer never considered himself a member of the art-for-art's-sake school.

Art's second danger—to the poet himself—testifies further to the urgency and importance of the creative act as Kipling envisioned it. When Lurgan Sahib says of Kim, himself a great artist in his own line, that "from time to time God causes men to be born—and thou art one of them— who have a lust to go abroad *at the risk of their lives* and discover news," his description may be taken as a metaphor for all creative men. All artists risk life, at one time or another, Kipling thought, in the hope of creating it; they hazard, if not their bodies, then their reputations, their comforts, their minds, their souls for the chance to "discover news" and to shape that news into patterns that will survive. And when one of those patterns does survive— when, for example, Apis, in a fine metaphor for immortality, passes out of the bullfighting arena by the very door through which he had entered—it becomes clear that art here is the most serious as well as the most dangerous of occupations.

Certainly, despite Kipling's reputation as a jingler and a polemicist, his total commitment to art can hardly be questioned in such a tale as "The Bull that Thought," and his sense of high purpose is perhaps most evident in the movement of the story—paralleling the development of the artistic consciousness—toward an ever more mystical experience. Craftsmanship, mere mechanism at the beginning of the tale, becomes transfigured in the final scene and reappears there as a rush of effortless creativity; the self-conscious technician has grown into "the true artist who knows he is but the vessel of an emotion whence others, not he, must drink." At the same time, brutality and gross self-centeredness become transmuted into the perfect mutual regard which makes possible the dance of life at the conclusion of the story, just as the "truculent mirth" of Apis, the killer, early in the tale becomes the "restorative hilarity" of Apis, the life-giver, at the end.

Kipling's own career, paralleling the career of Apis and the movement in the picture-frame of the story, developed through just these stages. First, there was the young writer, superbly endowed by nature and building an early reputation for himself upon his remarkable facility and his often cruel brashness. Next, there was the somewhat older Kipling, occasionally betrayed by his technical facility and his addiction to brutality, his callous practical joking, but sensing that these apparent liabilities might be converted to assets with luck and under just the right pressure of necessity. Finally, there was the old artist, the creator of such a story as "The Bull that Thought," a man whose craftsmanship had become intuitive and unself-conscious, whose mirth was now oftener creative than destructive, and who at long last had, in Edward Albee's words, "clawed his way to compassion."[15] Randall Jarrell, summing up Kipling's talent in a phrase which might refer to such stories as "The Wish House," "Dayspring Mishandled," and "The Gardener," but which especially characterizes "The Bull that Thought," speaks of "the exquisite tenderness that began in cruelty."[16] For Kipling, this is inevitably the direction which all art takes.

15. Quoted in the *New York Post* (November 6, 1962), p. 14.

16. Randall Jarrell, "On Preparing to Read Kipling," *A Sad Heart in the Supermarket* (New York, 1962), p. 128. Richard Le Gallienne, writing in 1900, saw Kipling as one of those influences specifically retarding the "great world movement . . . from brute force to spiritual enlargement." "The Bull that Thought" directly confronts this criticism and refutes it by showing such a movement to be of the very essence of Kipling's art.

CHAPTER SEVEN 🏵

"Kipling Suspected It"

i

In the course of my efforts in this study to try to hear and identify the voice of "the good Kipling," I have in passing had to consider a great deal of criticism of "the bad Kipling"—attacks on the author, for instance, for his complacency, his brutality, his superficiality, his imperialism, and so on. My response to this criticism has been quite deliberately to promote Kipling the artist above all the other Kiplings who have concerned readers through the years—Kipling the political figure, the cultural phenomenon, the psychological curiosity—and in particular to show how a great many of the extra-literary issues raised by discussion of these different Kiplings more properly belong under the heading of aesthetics. But study of a number of an author's individual works for the purpose of discovering the single, coherent voice which speaks in each of them inevitably raises the question of whether these works, when taken as a whole, also project a single, coherent voice; and here the value of insisting that for Kipling ideas proceed from art (instead of the other way around) becomes most clear.

Some of the earliest attempts by readers to characterize Kipling's voice illustrate very well the danger of basing judgments of art on certain *a priori* assumptions about the artist's ideas and attitudes. For example, when Kipling first began to make a name for himself in London in the eighteen-nineties, the element in his work that was most emphasized was its novelty. Everything about the young writer seemed new: his subject matter, his view of life, his style. One critic summed up this sense of novelty when he wrote that it was "one of Kipling's chief distinctions to have been able to see and feel romance without the aid of antiquity."[1] Yet this statement, with its oblique glance at the Aesthetics' already tiresome penchant for the Culture of the past ("Art stopped short/In the cultivated court/Of the Empress Josephine"), suggests very clearly the extent to which the case for Kipling's novelty was based on a misunderstanding by early readers both of their own times and of the writer's real concerns.

In the first place, Kipling was really a latecomer to the "romance of the here and now." England had been celebrating its material progress for decades before Kipling appeared. In 1851, the Crystal Palace had elevated mechanical contrivances to the rank of museum exhibits, with Poet Laureate Tennyson hymning

> Harvest-tool and husbandry,
> Loom and wheel and enginery. . . .

and even earlier, Wordsworth had sung the praises of "steamboats, viaducts, and railways." The idea was plainly in the air. Indeed, it was precisely this universal preoccupation with the bright new gadgets of industrial England which had inspired the Pre-Raphaelite return to the past. Kipling may have stepped onto the literary stage just in time to see Romance bring up the 9:15, but before that it had brought up the 8:15 and the 7:15 as well.

Moreover, if the times about which the young author wrote were not distant from his readers, the places and

---

1. Holbrook Jackson, *The Eighteen-Nineties* (London, 1913), p. 235.

people certainly were. Few Englishmen knew anything about India, or for that matter about Tommy Atkins, before Kipling's early work began to appear in Henley's *Scots Observer*, and so it was as much the exoticism of the far away as the romance of the here and now that accounted for the new writer's enormous popularity. And in this Kipling was only following another tradition. Oriental fads had swept England periodically for years. The eighteenth century had had an important literary revival of interest in the East, as had the Romantic Period, and the Aesthetic Movement itself, to which Kipling was supposed to stand in such contrast, was deeply involved with Japanese art and culture. More specifically, Robert Louis Stevenson, who immediately preceded Kipling as a popular literary figure and with whom the younger writer was often to be compared in later years, was a master of the adventure tale set in exotic places; so, for that matter, was Joseph Conrad, even then in process of writing his stories about distant continents and islands.[2]

---

2. Indeed, Kipling and Conrad were similar in many ways. They were both, though in different degrees, foreigners in England, and that foreignness, that double vision, so to speak, gave them a perspective on the country and a sense of its political and moral role in the world which other writers did not have or did not choose to make so much of. Then for both, the English language was—again in different degrees—a second tongue, one which had had more or less consciously to be learned and to the consequent special awareness of which can be laid, at least in part, another quality which the two men shared, stylistic brilliance and inventiveness and a concern for what sometimes seems pure verbal display. In subject matter they were also very close. Both dealt seriously with sensational materials, materials which forced them, all during their careers, to live down reputations as adventure story writers, and both sought to establish moral and ethical codes in their fiction, dramatizing the human condition in tales pitting men and women against the indifferent jungle, desert, and sea. Such a story as "The Man Who Would Be King," for example, is, in conception if not in execution, extremely Conradian, and such other works as "At the End of the Passage," "The Man Who Was," and "Without Benefit of Clergy" make use of elements which figure significantly in Conrad's own narratives.

Most damaging of all to Kipling's image as the foe of Aestheticism was the young author's spiritual kinship with aspects of the movement to which he reputedly stood opposed. Holbrook Jackson underscored one point of similarity between the two presumed antagonists when he spoke of how Kipling used his "rivals' " favorite weapons. "He knew what he thought and said what he thought in his own way, with as little apology to precedent or convention as the most ultra-realist or impressionist."[3] Just as important, Kipling's experiments with verse forms and his preoccupation with style also associated him, in spirit, with the writers of the Aesthetic Movement. True, one of his strident music hall ballads would have sounded strange on the lips of Oscar Wilde or Lionel Johnson, but his obsession with form and structure suggests a link with these men that may well have been quite as significant as the more obvious differences. His sestina was written in cockney dialect, but it was, nevertheless, a sestina.

Finally, the fact that Kipling's father was an artist, that his uncle was Burne-Jones, one of the great men of art in England, in whose house the writer-to-be was able to encounter casually such people as William Morris and the Rosettis, made devotion to a life of art almost inevitable for the young man. Later, he would use his youthful experiences as background for *The Light that Failed* and for such a story as "The Eye of Allah." More important, however, his early contacts with the artistic life—their naturalness and inevitability—helped to develop in him a wholly unself-conscious acceptance of the centrality of art, the very position toward which, in later years, many adherents of the Aesthetic Movement would have to struggle so deliberately and so painfully. Thus if Kipling never fell into

---

3. Jackson, p. 234.

any of the extravagances to which "art for art's sake" led in the period of the Nineties, neither did he doubt for a moment the absolute sovereignty of art in his life.

There were still other aspects of Kipling's subject matter and style which, though they struck early readers as startlingly fresh and new, were in fact parts of well-established traditions. For example, the author's verbal tricks, many of them catalogued by Leeb-Lundberg in 1909,[4] and such extraordinarily popular catch phrases as "but that's another story," helped at first to obscure the fact, quite apparent to later readers, of Kipling's great stylistic indebtedness to the Bible and to Elizabethan and Jacobean Literature. Moreover, many of the author's verse forms, seemingly so novel because so originally employed, were in reality the music hall ballads, the hymn tunes, and the banjo rhythms of contemporary popular music. What's more, beast fables had had an honorable history long before Kipling produced *The Jungle Books*, with the *Uncle Remus* stories a recent precursor; tales of the supernatural were, if anything, even more numerous; and soldier stories in dialect had an ancestry that could be traced back at least to Shakespeare's *Henry V*. Indeed, nearer to hand, as models for Kipling's dialect tales and for his use of local color were, in addition to *Uncle Remus*, the stories of Bret Harte, which the author had devoured avidly in his youth and which were extremely influential, and the works of Mark Twain, a man whom Kipling had long idolized.[5]

---

4. Leeb-Lundberg, *Word-Formation in Kipling* (Lund, 1909).
5. The careers of Mark Twain and Kipling ran strangely parallel. Both men came from provincial and, in the view of the literary world, exotic backgrounds, both learned the craft of writing on their own, in print shops and newspaper offices, and both, in their free use of unconventional material and in their brilliant and innovative handling of the language, helped to break down the genteel literary traditions of their day. There are many echoes of Mark Twain in Kipling, of which the insistence upon accuracy in dialect is only the most obvious. The adventures of boys, for

This accumulation of sources and analogues is intended to show how traditional were the elements of Kipling's art and not to detract from the author's very real originality. Kipling was original, as all fine artists are, not so much in his materials as in the uses he made of them, in the new relationships he was able to construct out of old experiences. The British had heard hymn tunes before, and they had also heard about their imperial responsibilities before. But they had never before heard them linked in the way Kipling linked them, and it was to the novelty and the vitality of this new arrangement of elements that they chiefly responded.

Against such a background as this, Holbrook Jackson's explanation of Kipling's sudden success in London is easily understandable. "Everybody felt," writes Jackson, "that a new force in a double sense had come into literature. It was a new voice, a new accent, in many ways a new language, and in every way forceful..."[6] But when, a moment later, Jackson adds that Kipling struck people as having had "no antecedents," we might well ask what had become of all the readers of Burns and Dickens and even Surtees in England. And when the historian goes on to say that "critics found it impossible to locate [Kipling], even when they admitted that he had earned a definite place in the hierarchy of art,"[7] we can only wonder at the difficulties

---

example, loom large in the works of both writers. Then, the emphasis which the older man placed on meticulous attention to craft—on doing the job well—markedly influenced Kipling and, in part through Kipling, such a later writer as Ernest Hemingway. Twain was aware of Kipling and his homage, and whenever he had reason to speak of the younger man, he always did so with great, if somewhat ironic, deference. "Between us," he said on one occasion; "we cover all knowledge. He knows all that can be known, and I know the rest."

6. Jackson, p. 232.
7. Jackson, p. 233.

early commentators seemed to face in their attempts to explain Kipling's appeal.

ii

The mistake these commentators made was to see such an extra-literary matter as Kipling's own personal youth and freshness as in some way epitomizing his art. Modern readers make the same kind of error when they assume that because Kipling has been around now for a long time and because many of the political views which he held (or is supposed, on the evidence of his poems and stories, to have held) seem to be as much a part of the dead past as the events which inspired them, he is himself an author who manifestly has no word for the twentieth century. In fact, just the opposite is true, and here we approach an answer to the question of where the real strength in Kipling's work lies and to what sort of audience he may be expected to appeal in future years. For if one fact recurs persistently in the analyses of texts in this study, it is that all of Kipling's best stories, however "old-fashioned" they may seem in superficial ways, embody a world view that speaks with especial force and relevance to the serious modern reader.

This is not to suggest that Kipling was a great or an original thinker. He did not have a particularly analytical mind, and it is significant that when Bonamy Dobrée undertook to discuss the source of the writer's strength as an artist, he spoke not of his philosophical grasp of, but rather of his "profound intuition"[8] into the loneliness of man confronting himself and the universe. That universe, as Kipling saw it, and as he expressed it in many of his stories, was the late nineteenth-century universe of accidental encounters and

---

8. Bonamy Dobrée, *Rudyard Kipling* (British Book Council: London, 1951), p. 7.

random violence which the author shared with nearly every other artist of the period. The philosophical climate of those years has often been discussed and analyzed. The times were characterized, as we know, by a breakdown of faith in old orders. Long-cherished economic, social, scientific, and religious theories and beliefs were being undermined by constantly expanding investigations into the nature of the material world, and the most far-reaching and unlooked for consequence of all this inquiry was intellectual uneasiness, a loss of faith in the old answers to perennial questions, notably in man's ability to control his life to any significant degree through his own actions, and, ultimately, despair. The harmony which had once existed between mankind and nature, John Ruskin wrote, making a metaphor of the 1883 eruption of Krakatoa, "is now broken and broken the world round: fragments, indeed, of what existed still exist, and hours of what is past still return; but month by month the darkness gains upon the day, and the ashes of the Antipodes glare through the night."[9]

This was the gloomy universe in which many thoughtful men lived at the end of the nineteenth century. Yet, if artists and philosophers were almost unanimous in their recognition of the unique problems which such a universe posed, no two of them seemed able to agree about how to deal with those problems; and thus, it was not so much Kipling's *acceptance* of the world picture of his day as his *response* to it which was recognized as special, which gave his utterances their characteristic vitality, and which, today, recommends his work to modern readers.

Indeed, of the many writers of the period—some of them Kipling's artistic superiors—who dealt directly with the problem of man trapped in an indifferent universe, a num-

---

9. John Ruskin, *Works,* ed. E. T. Cook and A. D. O. Wedderburn, XXXIV (London, 1902-1912), p. 78.

ber seem not to have been seriously concerned with the
matter of human response at all. The mere definition of
man's plight appears to have precluded, for these artists,
the possibility of meaningful reaction. Thomas Hardy, for
one, in his vision of man and man's spirit as playthings of
"purblind doomsters," seemed to confront a world essentially indifferent to human destiny. His *Jude the Obscure,
Tess of the D'Urbervilles,* and most notoriously *The Dy-
nasts* show "crass casualty" and not human will decreeing
the fate of mortals, and it is precisely in this mechanistic
determinism, in the inevitable impotence of his characters,
that he differs most sharply from Kipling. As Noel Annan
has written, "Kipling did not personify Nature like Hardy:
like a sociologist he took the environment as given and
noted its effect upon man."[10] And, we might add, refused
to prejudge what that effect might be. Thus, in the enig-
matic story "Mrs. Bathurst," set in a universe as fortuitous
and indifferent as any in Hardy's poetry or fiction, there
continues to be, at moments of crisis, and for every man,
a choice of action. Kipling's acceptance of this fact may
well have been as mystical, as irrational, as sentimental,
even, as Hardy's determinism. But when, in the story, he
has Pritchard ask "And if a man gets stuck with that kind
o' woman, Mr. Hooper?" and he has Hooper reply, "He
goes crazy—or just saves himself," he acknowledges the
existence of a meaningful choice of personal responses to
the universe, as Hardy does not, and takes—philosophically
—a position much more susceptible to development. For
though Hardy is without question a great artist—greater
than Kipling—and though he created some of the most
resonant metaphors for despair in all literature, his philosophy is to a large extent an intellectual dead-end. Like a

---

10. Noel Annan, "Kipling's Place in the History of Ideas," *Victorian
Studies,* III (June, 1960), 328.

latter-day Zeno, the poet and novelist tried to demonstrate, in the face of countless arrows reaching their targets every day, the impossibility of their doing so. It was inevitable, then, that his vision should have come to seem melodramatically limited to many of his readers, and his celebrated despair, like his abandonment of the novel form, a too-precipitate withdrawal from the fight.

Unlike Hardy, Joseph Conrad believed in the possibility of human response to the "absurd" universe, and in this belief he occupied a philosophical position closer to Kipling's than did most serious artists of the time. If the two writers were much alike in doctrinal terms, however, they differed importantly on at least one issue. For Conrad's response to the challenge of life was in essence an aristocratic one, while Kipling's remained, in spite of the author's apologies for colonialism, largely egalitarian. To put it another way, Conrad apparently felt that in a dark universe, some men have a greater obligation than others to penetrate the blackness, that some failures are more terrible than others; while Kipling's special gift was to recognize, and to place at the center of much of his best fiction, the idea that an obligation to moral consciousness is universal. For Kipling, in spite of such catch phrases as "the white man's burden," there was only one kind of challenge in the world and only one kind of failure. Thus if Ameera in "Without Benefit of Clergy" and Peroo in "The Bridge-Builders," as native Indians, and Holden and Findlayson in the same stories, as Englishmen, approached life from very different directions and with very different sorts of preparation, their responsibility to themselves was the same, and the failure of one would have been of exactly the same magnitude as the failure of the others. It is perhaps for this reason that there are no heroes or villains in Kipling's best work as there are in Conrad's; no moral aristocrats of whom much is expected and moral plebeians of whom nothing is expected—Lena and Heyst, on the one hand, Jones, Ricardo and Schomberg on the other. Indeed, it is very largely on this count that Charles Burkhart, in a recent essay,[11] ranks Conrad among the Victorian rather than among the modern novelists. And it is in this matter at least that Kipling, though he is Conrad's inferior in many ways, speaks more directly to us today than his contemporary does.

A number of writers of this same period did, of course, prescribe an active response to the universe that was not notably aristocratic. Browning's "Prospice," for example, Henley's "Invictus," Longfellow's "Excelsior," though they do not necessarily represent their authors at their best, do preserve for us one authentic note of the late nineteenth century, that shrill note of faintly hysterical heroism—forward to death, banners flying—which was the reaction of many men and women to the new chaos. This was action of a sort, a hold-over from the days when action had seemed really efficacious. It was not, however, in any sense creative action, action designed to achieve a constructive end. Nor is this fact surprising. For to many people living in the second half of the last century, the breakdown of the old order was not a challenge to be met and overcome but a disaster to be endured. They could conceive of nothing following that disaster, and so, like people moments before a crash, they braced themselves for the end and gave their thoughts up wholly to the matter of dying well. Thus it is no accident that the three poems are principally concerned with the problem of how to look good while being crushed. The self-conscious heroism of the pieces, their sententiousness, established immediately by the classical titles, and their theatricality all suggest the desperate poses of men who are about to die.

11. "Conrad the Victorian," *English Literature in Transition*, VI, 1 (1963), 1.

Kipling, on the other hand, does not, in his best work, seem someone braced for a crash so much as—to continue the metaphor—he appears to be someone who has been through a crash and who, miraculously, is still alive. The crash has been terrible; it has left him broken; things will never again be what they were—but he has survived it and indeed is even beginning to think about how to live and what to do in its wake. It is just in this casting about for some significant action to take, however, that he makes a curious discovery. He finds that the paralysis which had very naturally gripped everyone in those last days when the crash was so imminent has become institutionalized, has been elevated, as it were, to a philosophy, a philosophy whose first principle is the permanent futility of action. And thus, before he can act at all, it is necessary for him to try to discover the terms in which action may once more be meaningful for man, to redefine human freedom not in the old, comparatively naive pre-crash phrases, but in the light of the now firmly established post-disaster world.

iii

We have only to outline these problems of the man who has been through the crash to see how distinctly they are the very problems of the present day with which a number of contemporary artists and philosophers have struggled. Albert Camus, for one, created in his modern rendering of the story of Sisyphus a powerful symbol of man confronting the questions of freedom and action that have arisen from the disintegration of the old order in the nineteenth century. Not by chance is Sisyphus depicted as a man who has been through the crash. He need not have been so portrayed. A nineteenth-century determinist, for example, might easily have seen in this figure out of mythology a metaphor for man enslaved, the helpless plaything of the indifferent gods. A poet like Browning or Henley, on the

other hand, might have chosen to represent Sisyphus in
the moment when he first learns of his fate, contemptuous
of the forces that stand ready to destroy him and striding
without hesitation into eternity.

Characteristically, Camus confronts us with a Sisyphus
who has already been at his irrational stone-rolling for
millenia. That occupation has lost none of its madness over
the centuries, but one thing it *has* lost is its novelty. The
surprise and horror of learning what he must perpetually
suffer have worn off for Sisyphus, and he is very different
now from the man he was on that first day, full of foreboding about his doom but with no actual experience of it. (In
a way, this is the chief distinction between man before and
after the crash.) One difference which that experience—
and the consciousness of that experience—has made for
Sisyphus is to show him a way out; not a way out of the
absurdity by which he is surrounded, for no such escape
is possible, but a way out of his own personal commitment
to that absurdity.[12] All the while that he is straining to force
the great stone to the top of the hill (Camus shows us),
Sisyphus is wholly committed to the insanity of his world,
caught up, in spite of himself, in its mad laws. Indeed, the
stone is a metaphor for the burden of that madness, for
despair. The moment the boulder slips away from him,
however, and plunges back down the hill—the climax of
the torture for anyone genuinely interested in stone-rolling
—Sisyphus is temporarily released from his obligation to
irrationality. As he walks down the slope empty-handed
he is, Camus says, his own man. He returns to the fortress
of his own sanity, and for the time that it takes him to
reach the bottom of the hill, he is free.

Camus' definition of freedom is precise. In *The Myth of
Sisyphus* he says that there are two facts, and only two, that

---

12. In "Report to an Academy," Franz Kafka makes a similar point.

man can know for certain: one, that the human being longs
for order, and two, that he can never fully satisfy that longing in a world in which death, the executive arm, as it were,
of chaos, has the last word. Some men, Camus points out,
take the leap of faith; they yield to their desire for order
by imposing that order upon, and therefore willfully falsi-
fying their experience of, the absurd universe. Other men
commit suicide, driven to despair by their knowledge of
the madness of the universe, and failing to understand that
in their desire for order lies the means for achieving a personal freedom from that madness. Finally, there are those
men who succeed in winning their freedom, men who,
through an intense act of consciousness, acknowledge the
reality of the absurd universe, but recognize further its
irrelevance to their own existence. Sisyphus is such a man.
Walking down hill, he returns to the order and reality of
his own being (he had originally been doomed for a too-
great reverence for that being), and so is free of the absurd
universe in the only way—Camus would have us understand—that man has ever been or can ever be free. Hamlet
makes the same point when he cries

O God, I could be bounded in a nutshell and count myself a
king of infinite space, were it not that I have bad dreams. . . .

Freedom is a function not of the nutshell but of the dreams,
not of the externally imposed conditions of life but of the
level of consciousness of that life. Thus the freedom which
so many people of the nineteenth century felt they had
lost, and whose loss shattered their faith in the efficacy of
rational action, was, according to Camus, a freedom they
had never had, the freedom to ignore absurdity and despair. On the other hand, the freedom which they had always had (though they had not always exercised it), remained unchanged by the new scientific discoveries or the

semantics of particular philosophies. It was the freedom to understand their own natures and to fulfill themselves in their own terms.[13] The act of consciousness, then, the establishment of human experience as ultimately sovereign, is Camus' well-known response to the absurd universe.

iv

It is also Kipling's response in his most serious work, work spanning fifty years and touching on almost every possible subject. Nearly all his best tales, for example, are marked by what Bonamy Dobrée speaks of in *The Lamp and the Lute*, as "metaphysical scepticism . . . belief in the void which surrounds existence,"[14] and what C. S. Lewis calls "that bleak misgiving—almost that Nothingness."[15] That void, that nothingness, is at least in the background, and is very often central to the meaning of most of Kipling's writings. In such early tales as "The Arrest of Lieutenant Golightly" and "In the House of Suddhoo," simple anecdotes already darkened by hints of the unmanageability of things; in such late stories as "The Gardener" and "The Bull that Thought," in which the First World War is the entirely appropriate symbol of absurdity; in the helplessness of Vickery in "Mrs. Bathurst"; in the obsessiveness of Dowse, the mad "Disturber of Traffic"; in the terrible sandpit of "The Strange Ride of Morrowbie Jukes," Kafka-

13. It may be for this very reason that the Victorians took the "discovery" of the absurd universe so hard. In many important ways, the sexual being only the most obvious, they had rigorously suppressed their own natures, and so when the collapse of external order threw them back upon themselves they were horrified. The thought that life's purpose might after all be to fulfill their own natures in every particular must have seemed to some people in the late nineteenth century more terrible than the idea of no purpose in life at all.

14. Bonamy Dobrée, *The Lamp and the Lute* (London, 1964), p. 52.

15. C. S. Lewis, "Kipling's World," *They Asked for a Paper* (London, 1962), p. 92.

esque forerunner of the recent Japanese novel *Woman in the Dunes*; in the elaborate, mystical tale of the animal gods in "The Bridge-Builders"—again and again we are confronted with an irrational universe, indifferent to man but often deadly in its carelessness. The list could easily be extended to include some of the best-known of Kipling's stories: "Without Benefit of Clergy," "The Man Who Would Be King," "At the End of the Passage," "On Green-how Hill," "The Courting of Dinah Shadd," "Love-o'-Women," to select only a few at random. Indeed, these works all take their special color from the fact of impending and largely unavoidable disaster, and it is significant that in all of them the characters are represented to us as having attained varying levels of consciousness in response to the challenge of this disaster, and as having achieved varying degrees of freedom in proportion to that consciousness. Golightly, for example, and the narrator of "In the House of Suddhoo," being totally ignorant of the ways of the universe, are utterly victimized by chance. The former, with his dandy's wardrobe that makes no provision for bad weather, and the latter, with his misplaced confidence in the omnipotence of the British Raj, are examples of moral flotsam, controlled entirely by forces outside themselves, borne along on whatever currents they happen to blunder into. Ameera, on the other hand, the poised heroine of "Without Benefit of Clergy," and Apis, the masterful "thinking" bull, as they become more and more aware of their own natures and assume greater and greater control over them, become freer and freer of the absurd universe and find it growing constantly more irrelevant to their real existences.

Mere awareness of absurdity, however, is not enough to deliver man from despair. Such awareness, by itself, Camus characterizes as the prelude to suicide, to the profound nihilism, for example, of the late nineteenth century, and indeed, though such figures as Vickery, the pathetic victim of woman's love in "Mrs. Bathurst," and the prematurely buried Helen Turrell of "The Gardener" are conscious of the emptiness of their lives, that consciousness is not enough to turn them from the path that leads to self-destruction. What is required, then, in addition to consciousness, both writers tell us, is an active commitment to what that consciousness reveals; absurdity in the universe, but also the sense of order within the mind. What is required, in short, is the sort of Job-like affirmation of human experience in the face of the whirlwind which Camus sees in Sisyphus and which Kipling depicts in so many of his best stories. But such affirmation requires a tremendous act of will, a huge expenditure of psychic energy. And so Ameera, rejecting ritual and affirming the sovereignty of her own nature at the brink of death; Apis, cheating death with a burst of creativity, a perfect ordering of his experience; Findlayson, the bridge-builder, imposing his own vision of life upon the gods by main force of exhausting labor, subduing the violent Ganges with his bridge—all are very specifically characters in action, characters who have moved sufficiently beyond the mere awareness of life's absurdity to be able to act meaningfully in the face of it.

Kipling is not, of course, naive in his celebration of the efficacy of action; he does not, for example, ask us to return to a happier day when men believed they could physically vanquish the absurdity of the universe—and thus Findlayson's bridge is not offered as a physical victory over disorder (we are very clearly told that, as the gods measure time, the bridge will last only a moment), but rather as a symbol of the engineer's personal triumph, his assertion of his own reality as the only reality that matters. In the same way, Camus would have us recognize that Sisyphus' comparable achievement of freedom does not mitigate for an instant his obligation to roll his stone perpetually uphill, and that for him, as, for example, for Ameera, the process of growth and change must take place on an interior stage. Still, though action is, in the philosophies of both these writers, directed inward, not outward, it is action nonetheless and challenges, on Kipling's part with notable prescience, the paralysis of much late nineteenth- and early twentieth-century thought.

v

To account for an artist's special vision critics often turn to biography. Biography can deceive, of course, but it can also, by increasing the critic's confidence in his intuitions, by offering him, as it were, another avenue of approach to his subject's always ingeniously guarded secret, reinforce an insight already established by careful textual analysis, or at least offer a metaphor for that insight. About Kipling, for example, we might legitimately wonder how it happened that one man was able to see, where others were not, that the new conception of the universe emerging in his day was a condition, not a terminus, of civilization; how it was that that man particularly should have been capable of forcing his way through to the other side—our side—of late nineteenth-century desperation and of speaking to us, more clearly than many of his contemporaries, about our own relationship to that despair. For the beginning of an answer to this question, Kipling's biography is in many ways extremely enlightening.

Among the most crucial years in Kipling's life, as I noted in the last chapter, were those desolate ones between 1871 and 1876 which the boy spent far from his parents in a kind of foster home in England. It was the custom for Anglo-

Indians to send their school-age children home for their
education, and thus when Kipling was not yet six years old,
he and his sister were deposited with the family of a retired naval officer in Southsea. There, from his sixth to his
eleventh year, the young Rudyard was forced to endure
the inexplicable separation from his parents and, more immediately, the shame and degradation heaped on him in
the "House of Desolation." Those years have been well-
documented. Kipling himself spoke of them in detail in
his memoir *Something of Myself*, and used the same experiences, only partly disguised, in such fictional works as
"Baa, Baa, Black Sheep" and *The Light That Failed*. Moreover, critics have seen, in the agony of that childhood experience, a source of the anger and brutality which mar so
much of the author's fiction and verse, and Edmund Wilson in particular, tracing to that trauma in Southsea the
psychic wound he found in Kipling's character, called it,
as we have already seen, the shaping event of the artist's
life.

There is one curious fact about the whole Southsea episode, however, which is not often emphasized but which
emerges the moment the experiences of Kipling's early life
are set down baldly as Randall Jarrell has set them down
in the essay he called "On Preparing to Read Kipling."
"For the first six years of his life," Jarrell writes,

the child lived in Paradise, the inordinately loved and reasonably spoiled son of the best of parents; after that he lived in
the Hell in which the best of parents put him and paid to have
him kept. . . . At the end of six years the best of parents came
back for their leper . . . and for the rest of their lives they continued to be the best and most loving of parents.

Jarrell recognizes that his "best of parents" cannot help but
sound ironic, yet he insists that he does not mean the
phrase ironically at all.

From the father's bas-reliefs for *Kim* to the mother's "There's no Mother in Poetry, my dear," when the son got angry at her criticism of his poems—from beginning to end they were bewitching; you cannot read about them without wanting to live with them; they were the best of parents.

And then Jarrell comes to his point.

It is *this* that made Kipling what he was: if they had been the worst of parents, even ordinary parents, it would all have made sense, Kipling himself could have made sense out of it. As it was, his world had been torn in two and he himself torn in two. . . .[16]

In short, the most significant fact about the Hell which Kipling was forced to endure for five of his most impressionable years was that, in terms of any reasonable continuity, it had little or nothing to do with the rest of his experience.

Up to a point, Kipling's unlikely history parallels the intellectual movement of the nineteenth century, beginning in Eden ("Bliss was it in that dawn to be alive,/But to be young was very heaven . . ."); quickly plunging into Hell ("Month by month the darkness gains upon the day.") But where the century continued in despair to the end, even projecting its disillusion into our own time, Kipling was physically able to escape from his private torment. And though the knowledge of that torment's existence haunted him all his life, warping much of his nature and art, what he chiefly seems to have learned from his experience was that the Hell that gapes for every man need not, for all its horror, define his life. Hardy's characters are for the most part defined by—are chiefly functions of—the indifferent universe in which they live. In the same way, the figures in

---

16. Randall Jarrell, "On Preparing to Read Kipling," *A Sad Heart in the Supermarket* (New York, 1962), pp. 129-130.

"Prospice" and "Invictus," for all that their heads are bloody but unbowed, expend their energies reacting to the absurdity of life and thus, in spite of themselves, are shaped by what they most despise, their only victory a hollow one, contempt for the bully cosmos even as it strikes them down.

Kipling, on the other hand, perhaps influenced by the events of his childhood, believed profoundly, like Camus, in the possibility of escape, not of escape from the *influences* of the absurd universe—every life, his best stories show, must be played out against that background—but of escape from the need to spend life *reacting* to that absurdity. Specifically, from his (intellectual) recognition that the five years he had spent in Hell were really extraneous to the rest of his experience, came the definition of human freedom which, though he was largely incapable of implementing it in his own life, he embodied movingly in such a story as "Without Benefit of Clergy." There, Ameera and Holden learn that ritual, because it is merely a slavish reaction to the irrational universe, is for that reason a surrender to it; that by thus giving up their initiative, they have in effect given up their own natures, their freedom. It is only when they make this discovery—the crucial moment of growth and change in the story—that they decide to reject ritual:

They sat together and laughed, calling each other openly by every pet name that could move the wrath of the gods. . . .

decide to act, like Sisyphus, independently of the absurd and to create a kind of enclave of sanity in life on their own terms.

The origin of Kipling's belief in the feasibility of escape, in the possibility of changing one's condition through action, is again to be found, at least in part, in his biography. For surely, the young Rudyard's dramatic rescue from the private Hell of his Southsea days must have made almost as profound an impression on the boy as his original plunge into it. His mother had arrived without warning from India, we learn from *Something of Myself*.

She told me afterwards that when she first came up to my room to kiss me goodnight, I flung up an arm to guard off the cuff I had been trained to expect. I was taken at once from the House of Desolation, and for months ran wild in a little farmhouse on the edge of Epping Forest. . . .

The magical sense of release here is overwhelming; we can almost hear in it Defoe's astonished verse:

> A dreadful plague in London was
>   In the year sixty-five,
> Which swept an hundred thousand souls
>   Away; yet I alive!

It is this sense of having passed through Hell and emerged on the other side which makes this experience of Kipling's so central to his vision of life; that unique sense of having survived a fatal accident which enables him to speak to modern readers—who have also, miraculously, survived the first paralyzing impact of the same sort of accident—in a way that some of his contemporaries, still occupied with the absurd universe as an *impending* disaster, are not able to do. And what he is able to say to those readers, what, in his best work, he says with narrative force and clarity (for it is in his ability to give these ideas literary expression that his real importance lies), is first, that man is alone in a blank cosmos where he is ruled by impersonal Law; second, that through a highly conscious act of commitment to the reality of his own experience he can rescue himself from life's irrationality; and finally, that by doing this he secures for himself a meaningful freedom, albeit within the larger framework of the absurd. It is to twentieth-century readers who think of issues and responses such as these as central to an understanding of their age that the voice of "the good Kipling" speaks most powerfully today, and to whom it is likely to go on speaking for many years to come.

INDEX